The Sexual Alarm System

The Sexual Alarm System

Women's Unwanted Response to Sexual Intimacy and How to Overcome It

Judith Leavitt, EdD

JASON ARONSON
Lanham • Boulder • New York • Toronto • Plymouth, UK

Published by Jason Aronson
A wholly owned subsidiary of The Rowman & Littlefield Publishing Group, Inc.
4501 Forbes Boulevard, Suite 200, Lanham, Maryland 20706
www.rowman.com

10 Thornbury Road, Plymouth PL6 7PP, United Kingdom

British Library Cataloguing in Publication Information Available

Library of Congress Cataloging-in-Publication Data

Leavitt, Judith, 1946–
The sexual alarm system : women's unwanted response to sexual intimacy and how to overcome it /
Judith Leavitt.
  p. cm.
Includes bibliographical references and index.
ISBN 978-0-7657-0915-8 (cloth : alk. paper) — ISBN 978-0-7657-0916-5 (electronic)
1. Women—Sexual behavior. I. Title.
HQ29.L385 2012
306.7082—dc23
2012002406

♾™ The paper used in this publication meets the minimum requirements of American
National Standard for Information Sciences Permanence of Paper for Printed Library
Materials, ANSI/NISO Z39.48-1992.

Printed in the United States of America

To all the wonderful women
who have opened their hearts and shared their stories with me.
Thank you for your courage and for all that you have taught me.

Contents

Acknowledgments

I want to give a special acknowledgment to Sylvia Cohen who started me on this journey. To all who knew her, she was a pioneering spirit in the field of sex therapy. She was my guiding light.

Through over twenty years I have had the privilege of being part of a peer support group of fellow sex therapists. Many thanks to Rosalie Brown, Patty Buttner, Arthur Cobb, Joyce Friedman, Aurelie Goodwin, Kathleen Logan Prince, Judy Silverstein, and Richard York for your wonderful support, ideas, advice, and insights that you have shared with me.

Special thanks to Raquel Perlis and Margie Green for sharing of our clients and tackling some of the difficult issues about women's sexuality together.

A deep thanks goes to Dean Abby, Director of Continuing Education at the Massachusetts School of Professional Psychology, for giving me the opportunity to teach about women's sexuality. He has strongly supported the importance of students and professionals learning about human sexuality. Special thanks too to Stan Berman, Dean of Programs of Advanced Graduate Study, and Alan Beck, Dean of the Clinical Psychology Department, for their support for my teaching and their respect for this work.

Special thanks to my editor, Amy King, for her belief in my book and helpful direction.

I also want to acknowledge the great support of my partner, George Hecker, through this writing and publishing process. He helped me with his input, support, patience, and insights.

I want to thank my women friends who have shared this journey of being women together. And finally I want to thank my daughter for giving me a firsthand view of what it is to grow up being female.

Introduction

The Sexual Alarm System

My roommate was shaken up. She had been walking to work at 6:45 in the morning on the side streets of a "safe" neighborhood, our neighborhood. She was still waking up with a mug of coffee in hand. All of a sudden she felt something in a place where it shouldn't be. What was that? A hand coming from behind between her legs. She spun around quickly to see a man pulling a glove on his hand as he ran down a side street. Creepy! Rattled she quickened her pace to catch the bus. Once at work, she forgot about the incident. Yet, back at home telling us about what happened, she felt shaky, as did we all. From then on she found a different way to go to catch the bus, frequently looking around as she walked briskly. We all then watched around us as we walked through our neighborhood.

As a young sex therapist I kept hearing stories like this. It amazed me how pervasive scary incidents like this were for girls and women. As a young girl playing in the park, Janine walked by a car parked at the edge of the green. As she went by, a man opened his door and she saw something strange sticking up from his pants. She had never seen something like this and didn't know what it was, but she was scared and ran to her mother, never revealing what had happened. How did she know to be scared? How did she know not to tell? Why did she not like that park so much anymore?

One morning in my thirties, I had an incident of my own. Not that I hadn't had things happen before. But, now I was aware. I knew how common these things were. Yet, my awareness didn't stop my heart from pounding, didn't stop me from fleeing. Perhaps I should have screamed or called the police, but you don't think of those things then. You just want to get to safety. It was 6:45 a.m. on a warm sunny Sunday summer morning, my favorite time to run. It was just before the heat of the day settled in and there was still some cool. The world was quiet and serene. I had it all to myself. Or so I thought. As I set out on my run, I drank in the balminess and the quiet. I headed up my usual route on the main road, not a very large road. Ahh! No one was out yet. I settled into a comfortable pace, letting myself feel a reverie coming over me. Then, strangely, a car went by. It was pretty early on a Sunday morning for a car. Yet, I'd seen some before on my run. I let it go. A few minutes later, another car went by in the other direction. Wait a minute, wasn't that the same car? Who was in it? One person? Yes. A man? I thought so. I began to get nervous. But, I said to myself that perhaps he couldn't find where he was going. Or maybe he did an errand and was going back. Now, however, I was on alert. My eyes were glued to the road. Then to my horror came a third car. This time it was definitely that blue car that had already gone by once, twice. This time, I didn't wait a second to find out more. As fast as my legs would carry me, I ran into someone's back yard and tried to disappear up the yards into some bushes. Surely he couldn't find me there since there was no road. But what if he got out and was on foot. How was I to get home without going back on the road? I made it home and I never went out running that early on a Sunday morning again.

How many of us have had these experiences? Nothing really awful happened. Or did it? Of course many awful things do happen to many women. And for the few women who haven't had these experiences, they know they are right outside the door because they have been taught, they listen to the news, their sisters have stories.

This book is about how experiences like these affect a woman's sexuality. It is about how girls learn from a young age that they are not safe because they are female. It is about how this lack of safety affects our lives, our bodies, and our relationships. Something happens to us that changes us, that induces fear in us and that separates us from ourselves and our bodies. I give this phenomenon a name, the Sexual Alarm System, and I discuss how it works in our lives. Then I look at how to heal and I develop a series of exercises to help bring women back to their bodies and expand their physical experiences. The exercises are a centerpiece of the book offering women a new and unique way to heal and find connection to their sexuality.

No one has written a book quite like this that describes the Sexual Alarm System (SAS) and gives ways to work with these kinds of specific body movements to help women find a path back to their bodies and their sexuality. My goals are to validate what every woman knows and goes through, to give women a greater understanding of how we got here, and to offer women and the professionals who work with them new and critical tools for healing. In my therapy practice and in workshops I run, I have seen how cathartic, joyful, releasing, and empowering this work can be. Over and over women cry when I describe the SAS to them. I have seen the look of amazement when women come back to a session having done an exercise like Total Body Shaking that launches them into a new connection to their bodies. It gives me great joy to share an important part of my life's work through this book and to imagine more women understanding their makeup and doing exercises such as Vibrating, Shaking, Rolling, and Rocking. Through these exercises, I believe women will both break through the constraints that their SASs put around them and find new energy within themselves. These experiences have been critical for so many women in their journeys.

This is a book for all mental health professionals who work with women: sex therapists, psychologists, social workers, pastoral counselors, marriage and family counselors, mental health counselors, psychiatrists, etc. Whether or not they work directly with sexual issues, all mental health professionals need to understand the Sexual Alarm System and how profoundly it affects women. It is not only women's sexuality that is affected, but their whole being. The exercises presented here are designed to fill in a gap of available behavioral tools for helping women connect to their sexuality. The approach is unique in the way it helps women to connect to their bodies. The book is also for women who want to understand the SAS and work with the exercises on their own. For professionals who give these exercises to clients, it is very important that you try the exercises yourselves. In order to know what a woman client might experience in doing the exercises, you need to know what you experience. Do the exercises once, twice, and more. Enjoy them and use them for your own growth too.

THE CHAPTERS

Part I is about understanding the Sexual Alarm System. It contains three chapters.

Chapter 1 defines the phenomenon, which I call the Sexual Alarm System (SAS), looking at what it is and how it works. The chapter also explores the impact of the SAS on the whole of women's lives, the importance of men's lack of experience of the SAS, the experience of women who relate to women partners, and the Four Steps of Sexual Healing for women.

Chapter 2 goes into more depth looking at what triggers the SAS from two approaches: 1) categories of behaviors related to a woman's experiences, such as impersonal forceful behaviors, and 2) specific violations that trigger the SAS, such as unexpected movements and/or touch.

Chapter 3 reviews significant physiological background that gives the context for and explanation for the SAS. The chapter discusses the importance of instincts, the fight/flight response, and Daniel Goleman's work on the role of the amygdala, the neural chemical alerting system and emotional memory. Each of these helps explain how the SAS exists and functions and how it is not under a woman's control. Learning about this is a relief for many women.

Part II looks at background for the Sexual Alarm System. It contains four chapters.

Chapter 4 reviews the history of women's sexuality beginning with classical history through early Christian times into the Renaissance and Reformation and up into modern history. The long-held views of the inferiority of women and the danger of their sexuality are presented along with the extreme measures to control women from discovering and expressing their sexuality.

Chapter 5 presents a brief history of sex therapy to give a theoretical background to the material in this book. It establishes where my book fits into known sex therapy approaches, particularly that of Rosemary Basson. In addition, the chapter presents background on treatment approaches to working with women's sexuality, looking at how this book is similar to and different from important previous works.

Chapter 6 discusses the sexual development of girls, looking at the ways girls are at once controlled, oversexualized, and dissociated from their bodies in ways that contribute to the SAS. It brings in issues from the psychology of girls and women.

Chapter 7 describes additional issues that cause women's fear of their sexuality. Included are the following issues: family history, medical issues, lesbianism and bisexuality, and multicultural views of women's sexuality.

Part III addresses ways of working with the SAS. It contains chapters 8 through 12.

Chapter 8 looks at ways to go around the SAS. There are windows for women that are not wired with the Alarm. This chapter explores what these windows are and how to find them. Chapter 9 is for therapists in addressing men. It helps therapists speak directly to men about the SAS, explaining what it is and how it affects both their women partners and them.

Chapters 10 through 12 introduce exercises for therapists to help women learn how to be in their bodies and gain control of the Sexual Alarm System. Chapter 10 introduces the exercise programs that follow in the next two chapters. Chapter 11 describes a central way for women to deal with the Sexual Alarm System: that is to help them experience the dimensions of the sexual experience that are crucial to sexuality without the sex. I call this The Ingredients. It involves taking women through various physical aspects of the sexual experience without the sexual arousal. Learning to open the body in various ways without arousal means that the SAS is not likely to get triggered. Therapists can help women learn many of the aspects of being sexual that are essential to the experience without the scary and difficult parts.

In chapter 12 I develop the Progressive Exercises. In addition to the Ingredients, there needs to be an order of progression of body experiences that allows women to open up and take in the Ingredients. This progression needs to proceed through successive steps that gradually help women to experience their bodies more fully. These steps include: Awakening, Awareness, Allowing, and Surrender. In each step numerous exercises are presented for therapists to suggest to women clients. In addition, the chapter gives examples of a selection of exercises from each step connecting one to another and creating a flow from step one through four.

Part IV explores working with the SAS beyond the basic exercises. It includes chapters 13 through 16.

Chapter 13 shows how couples can use the exercises from the previous two chapters. Exercises from the Ingredients and the Progressive Exercises are adapted for couples to use together with the goal being to help women move around, through, and/or beyond the SAS.

Chapter 14 discusses a crucial step: how to add subjective arousal into the above experiences toward becoming sexual. The chapter presents how to do this carefully and sensitively in order to not trigger the SAS. Exercises for therapists to suggest to women alone and for couples are given.

Chapter 15 looks at ways for therapists to work directly with the SAS when women have significant emotional blocks that obstruct their healing progress. In addition to the exercises given in this book, a woman may need to directly confront issues and emotions that contribute to creating the SAS. Techniques such as Telling the Stories, expressing the fear, cognitive behavioral approaches, and Model Mugging are described.

Chapter 16 gives a summary of the book plus explores other approaches to dealing with the SAS. There are many exciting programs dedicated to helping girls and women with such issues as sexual violence, sex education, eating disorders, and men's support of women's sexual safety. The chapter presents descriptions of selected programs that address vital issues that contribute to the necessity of the SAS.

I

Understanding the Sexual Alarm System

Chapter One

What Is the Sexual Alarm System?

"I can't stand it when the first thing he does is grab my breasts."

"I hate it when he comes up from behind me."

"I flinch when she grabs me on the butt."

As a young therapist I noticed that I kept hearing these exclamations coming from women. Sometimes the words were exactly the same. I thought, "What is going on here?" I began to understand that the women were experiencing flinching, startle, fear, anger, anxiety. Often it was their loved one, someone they trusted, who elicited this response. I wondered why someone trusted would elicit such strong negative reactions? There had to be something deeper and more primal occurring. The women felt in danger, yet there was no danger present. How did woman after woman experience this and where did they learn this?

I developed a name for what I was hearing: The Sexual Alarm System. This chapter defines this Sexual Alarm System (SAS) and the four steps of how it operates. Further it looks at how the Alarm affects many aspects of women's lives, men's lack of experience of this Sexual Alarm, how the Alarm functions with women partners, and the Four Steps of Sexual Healing.

DEFINITION

What is happening inside of the woman? Something she has learned from a very young age. "Watch Out!" "Be Careful!" "Stop!" "What is Happening to me!" "It's my Responsibility!" One day when my daughter was three, I was standing in a grocery line with her. She was looking particularly cute, blonde and curly-haired. A man came up behind her in line, looked at her, looked at me, and said to me in a stern tone of warning, "You're going to have to

1

Watch Out for her when she grows up!" What is the message here . . . to a three-year-old? Being a girl makes her vulnerable! She'll need protection because she'll be in danger. What does she learn from the man? FEAR. "There Is Something Wrong with ME!" How incredibly sad! How infuriating to me as her mother. These messages go in at a deep visceral level.

And what is it that she has to fear? It is that she is prey. Her cuteness makes her prey. Her girlness makes her prey. And when she grows up, her womanness makes her sexual prey. So, she learns from the well-meaning (?) man, as she continues to do for the years to come, that she has to protect/hide something about herself. Yet, what she has to hide is the very thing that draws attention to her. So, in fact, she begins the long process of internalizing that she has to look a certain way to get attention, but she has to guard against the very attention she seeks even as she is getting it. The best way to adapt to that conundrum is to look a certain way, but not experience the feelings that are supposed to go with the look because the feelings are dangerous and besides, you have to spend your energy protecting yourself from the attention you seek because the attention is desired but dangerous! Whew! And she was only 3. As a woman, I recognize the long road of learning ahead. It is one I have internalized well. We call it socialization.

My daughter's cultural education about her sexuality continued. At a party when she was 13, two men I knew came up to me separately at differ-ent times and said the exact same words. My daughter was looking beautiful in a long gown in her budding development. The men said to me, "You're going to have to put her in a cage when she grows up." IN A CAGE! NO! NOT MY DAUGHTER! Can't I save her from this? Haven't I been teaching her to be proud of herself as a girl and to enjoy her developing sexuality? What is this? She, like all of us, must guard against THESE guys. My friends! Creepy! They are forty-year-old men. I can't protect her from this fear. In fact, she better know about it to protect herself. And then there is the insidious message, the not so hidden message that it is perhaps her own desires, her own sexuality that could be out of control and dangerous.

I want her to be free and to enjoy her womanhood as she grows up.

What is this cage that the men refer to? The cage is what I call the Sexual Alarm System. It is like a house alarm. Girls develop a body sensor for sexual danger: an unwanted hand, a look, a comment. What woman when walking out into a parking lot at 11 o'clock at night doesn't go into alert? What men are out there? How are they dressed? How close are they? Where are my keys? This is survival. This response is necessary to protect oneself. As women we all have stories: the hand pressing too close on the subway, the man following you on the street, the cat calls, the suspicious car too close. Harmless? At least some of it? No. Because behind it is the threat. How do you know when the threat is real? Many women have stories of being touched, threatened, forced. Always there is the ultimate fear: sexual assault.

It is surprising how many women have experienced incidents that solidify the SAS. These experiences are so common that many women consider them part of life. They move on unaware of the effect on their sense of sexual safety. Here is a short list of the types of incidents that occur every day for women.

A man looks you up and down.
A man says, "Hey baby, you're lookin' good!"
In a crowd you feel a hand graze you in a private place.
A store clerk asks if you have a boyfriend.
A truck driver toots and follows you.

HOW DOES IT WORK?

So how does the Alarm work? First of all, women are wired. This is the process that takes place as a result of growing up hearing comments like, "Put her in a cage." There are many more situations that let a girl know she must watch out. The boy on the school bus sneaks his hand into a girl's panties. The sixth grade boyfriend pushes oral sex on a female classmate. An uncle tells dirty jokes. A girl's Dad looks at porn secretly so her Mom doesn't know, but the daughter finds it. At school Noelle is called a "slut" because she has big breasts. A sister has to be home earlier than her younger brother because she is female. If a girl gets pregnant, she better not come home. A man exposes himself to Jeanette in public. It is all too familiar. And yet, it still goes on and on. Men are arrested. The boy on the bus is called to the principal's office. The mother drags the father to therapy. And yet, it goes on and on. Women's wiring is well cemented early on. It gets constant reinforcement. Where are the signals that a woman can be proud of being a sexual being, that she can enjoy her sexuality?

Darlene has had any number of encounters that have her wired. Ramon came on too strong. The boss at work made sexual innuendos. Around men she felt uneasy and uncertain. She grew up being told to watch out for boys who want to get into her pants.

Secondly, something happens. The SAS is like a house alarm ready to go off. Something crosses the boundary and the Alarm is triggered. Women are so used to their boundaries being violated that they may not even know it is happening. They think it is normal . . . because it is, after all, the norm. The response becomes instinctive. The guy in the parking lot who looks at a woman too long may trigger the Alarm. Or he may be looking at another woman too long and she gets triggered because it could be her. Women identify with each other. We are in this together.

One day Darlene walked by someone who looked like an old boyfriend, one who had intimidated her and pushed her too much sexually. The boyfriend had kept showing up in her life unwanted. Then the man walking by stared at her. Her SAS started shrieking. Danger!

Thirdly, after the Alarm is triggered, the woman goes into high alert. She is ready. She is watching, searching. Her antennae are up. Anything that resembles an Alarm trigger will be spotted. Her adrenaline is pumping. Her senses are acute. She is like a cat ready to spring. Often the woman doesn't even know she is triggered. Because she is so used to this reaction, she is not aware of her hyperreactivity. Because she is unaware, she may react to something in a way that doesn't make sense to her and/or her partner. For example, she may get irritated that he changed the TV station when she is really reacting to his hand on her inner thigh.

Now Darlene was on high alert. She ducked into a building to get rid of the staring man. Then she watched all around her as she continued walking. Her eyes were like radar. When getting in her car, she peered all around. Later that night when her fiancé, Baron, reached out to touch her in bed, she tensed up.

Simultaneously with her high alert state, the woman may go into action depending on the situation. She may slap away a hand, turn away, groan, tense, quicken her pace, flinch, etc. She may grab her keys, lock the doors, hide in the closet, run into the neighbor's yard to get away from the car that has passed by three times. She may cover her body. She wishes she could hiss, punch, give him the finger, call him out, tell him off. Sometimes she does speak up. Most of the time she tries to get out of the situation as fast as possible. It is not safe to stand up for herself. He is stronger, more aggressive, more demanding. Imagine if she were to turn to the guy on the street and say, "Hey you, get out of my face!"

Fourthly, she withdraws and shuts down. She turns off any possibility of a sexual response. This is so important for partners to realize. Their Alarm triggering approaches don't work. They get the opposite response from what they want. So, why do male partners persist? They often feel helpless to get any positive response from the woman so they figure they might as well keep trying something. The sun, the moon, and the stars have to be lined up perfectly. Maybe this is the night. Maybe one out of a hundred times, she will respond positively, so I'll keep trying. It is the old situation that random reinforcement creates a response that is the hardest to extinguish.

Withdrawing can take many forms. The woman physically and emotionally pulls away. Her skin becomes tighter. Her breathing becomes shallower. Her body becomes cooler, her tone duller, her voice flatter, her movements more constrained. She may become busier, more tired, more irritable. She talks a lot about other things . . . or her answers become shorter. She may retreat to the cat, the children, email. Partners know the signs and become more frustrated . . . and resigned.

Shutting down begins. The curtain drops. She is signing off. The door closes and she is gone deep inside. Self-esteem drops. Her body becomes heavy. She eats more or she eats less. She stops fixing her hair as often. The life energy is draining as she becomes more diminished. She has lost some of her vibrancy and her power. What a tragedy! Find a woman at the park or in the grocery store who is connected to her body and her sexuality. Compare her to the majority who are not. You will see the difference.

Another night Darlene's fiancé, Baron, came into the bedroom naked with an erection. Darlene jumped out of the bed yelling, "What are you doing?" Baron looked stunned. Embarrassed, he covered himself and went into the bathroom. Her heart beating, Darlene fell into a chair lost and over-whelmed. Later when Baron tried to talk with her about what had happened, Darlene could feel the wall closing in. Numbness. Through the fog she could barely hear him saying that he thought he would surprise her and turn her on. He was so sorry. She couldn't respond.

So, both are caught in a trap. She doesn't know what is happening and blames herself or maybe him. He doesn't know what is happening and blames her—or maybe himself. She is scared and angry, but experiences shame. He feels rejected and hurt which usually comes out as frustration and anger. She becomes the cold, unavailable wife. He becomes the sex-deprived husband. In her high alert state the woman may ignore her partner, snap at him, flinch, or put him down, treating him like he is an animal.

It happens to women partners also. Lauren hated being kissed. Deborah loved kissing and was distraught at Lauren's rejection. When Deborah ap-proached her to give her even a peck on the cheek, Lauren would pull back as if startled. She hadn't thought about why she did this. She just knew she felt unsafe and violated. As we looked through her history, she was able to describe two boyfriends in high school who liked big wet kisses over her whole mouth. Neither had paid attention to her avoidance of these kisses. Neither had honored her clear dislike of these kisses.

Some women push themselves through the Alarm System. This is one way, the least effective way, to deal with it. For many women, it is the only way they know. This involves 1) trying to ignore this triggered state, which is now on high alert, or 2) shutting down the Alarm experience and trying to become sexual anyway. Sounds intense. Sounds like the opposite of pleasur-able. It is! It is work. How do women do it? They make themselves. They may rationalize that this is for him or her or that, even though they won't get anything out of it for themselves, it helps the relationship or keeps the partner happy. So, in fact, they may go through with acting sexual and, at best, get nothing out of it, and, at worst, be miserable. Sometimes physical stimulation

by the partner creates arousal that supersedes the alarm. The woman is pro-
pelled into an excited sexual state that overrides her primal protective instinct. This can lead both partners to think, "Just do it and it will be OK." So
the woman gets excited, maybe has orgasm, gets some pleasure. Things are
all right, right? Not when the woman feels badly after. Not when the sexual
experience gives her no sense of well-being. Not when afterward she does
not absorb what has happened and may, in fact, want to forget it. Why do
these reactions happen? Because after it's over, the residue of the Alarm
comes back. It wasn't dismantled, it was overwhelmed. Now when the sexual
experience is over, aspects of the Alarm may return. The primary experience
is that nothing has changed for the next time around. The sexual experience
is not integrated, the Alarm is not dealt with. Men and women wonder why
these experiences don't help, why they don't prove to the woman that she can
be sexual, that her hesitations, resistance, and fears are not warranted. Why?
Because they don't address the Alarm.

If Carmen can just get by that apathy and sometimes dread. If she can just
push through it! If she can stick with it and not give up, she can finally feel
some arousal with enough clitoral stimulation. Evan keeps telling her to hang
in there. Then the arousal takes over and her body goes into spasms of
reactions. Pleasure? She wouldn't really describe it that way. Accomplish-
ment is more like it. She did it. Then she is done and wants to get on to her
day. The next time it will be the same.

THE SAS AND WOMEN'S LIVES

The SAS affects not only a woman's sexuality. It affects her whole life often
in ways that she has forgotten or takes for granted. Most women do not go
out into the night alone. So what if they need to be out at night? How do they
do it? Very carefully! They think through where they are going. They drive
there and figure out ahead of time where to park and how to walk to where
they are going. They may meet other women or be escorted by a man. So,
women lose the night! That is one consequence. Travel is another way wom-
en are affected. How many women would take off alone for a ride across the
country? A few. Most would go with friends or a man. Women who travel
alone on business are usually very concerned about where they are staying,
where the room in the hotel is located, who is around them when they go to
their room. Cars are another area. Women want reliable cars so they don't
end up stuck in an unsafe area or broken down at night. Thus, freedom is a
major area of a woman's life that is affected. Where can she go, when can
she go there, how does she get there? If a woman is single, where she lives is
very affected by her SAS. Many women living alone, or even with a partner,

don't want to live on the street floor of a building. If a woman lives in a whole house, she often makes sure that the windows are locked at night. (In fact, if her partner is a male, he will often make fun of her sense of safety about this and other things.)

Women get used to these things. So what else is affected? The list is long: how she dresses, how she wears her hair, how she acts at work, how she responds to male coworkers' innuendos, who she sits next to on the train, how she interacts with the man at the store counter, who is in the elevator as she enters, when she is alone with the male doctor. There are not many areas of her life that are not affected. The SAS alerts her and protects her regularly. It is so automatic that she doesn't think about it most of the time. All these things are part of life, aren't they? Yes. But not for men. Most men don't have to worry about how their sexuality puts them in danger.

MEN'S LACK OF EXPERIENCE OF THE SEXUAL ALARM SYSTEM

This is key: men do not experience the SAS. They don't know what is happening and they don't understand. Men are not in danger of sexual assault from women. (When I say this to heterosexual couples, some men say, "I wish.") Men do not walk around having to worry about being followed or sexually assaulted by a woman. Men may fear being mugged or beaten up by another man, but this is not sexual and it is not by a woman. These concerns do not produce a Sexual Alarm System. It is not in the man's experience to know what it is like to be on high protective alert about being a sexual being. What man worries if he gets in a subway car and the only other person there is a woman? What man feels scared if he is in a restaurant and discovers that a woman is looking at him? How many newspaper stories do we see in a day about a woman raping a man? It may even be hard to imagine how such an event could take place.

It is difficult to comprehend an experience that you have not had. White people rarely worry that the color of their skin may put them in danger. Tall men don't experience the struggle that short men often feel. It is important for men to understand their lack of experience of sexual fear. To understand their female partners, they need to put themselves in a woman's shoes. Imagine if they could go through the day as a woman. Two men have related to my description of the Sexual Alarm System. One man in a class I was teaching described that he knew what I was talking about. He said that he had an Alarm System that was around him all the time because he could be called names, attacked, even sexually assaulted. He was African American. Another man had worked for some years with primarily gay men. He often felt the same feelings women feel around heterosexual men. Men can act toward other men the way they do toward women. One group of men who do understand is men who have been sexually abused. They have a strong SAS.

Once the SAS is triggered, the woman shuts down sexually. So, while the woman's partner is trying to get her interested in physical closeness and sex, he may in fact be creating the opposite reaction: she shuts down and withdraws. It is essential for men and women to understand how the Sexual Alarm System works and it is critical to understand that it is not personal. Partners do take it personally and why not? They are getting pushed away. What develops may be a power struggle where she is the rejecter and the partner is the rejected. Yet, the issue may well not originate in their personal relationship because it is about sexual safety and survival. It is incredibly helpful for couples to understand this, to depersonalize this, and to be on the same side together.

Many men do not participate in the behaviors that scare women. They are also, in a sense, victims of these behaviors. Male partners feel angry that they have to pay the price of the actions of other men. "But, I don't act that way. I am her husband. Why can't she see the difference?" It is, in fact, unfair to men as well as women! It shows how men and women suffer from the permission that our culture (and many cultures) gives for male behavior toward women. Understanding this can help partners be together in dealing with the SAS.

Josh kept saying to Michele, "But I'm not like those guys. Why do I have to pay for what they have done?" Michele felt angry that he did not understand her experience. His attitude only distanced her further. When I introduced the concept of the SAS to them, both were better able to understand each other. It helped Josh enormously that Michele could see how unfair the SAS was not only to her, but also to him. He had tried very hard to be a good lover and meet her needs.

Chapter 9 helps therapists address men with the above issues. In my practice I often speak to men directly about the SAS and about themselves. Chapter 9 will help you as a professional find ways to talk with your heterosexual male clients.

WOMEN PARTNERS

When the partner is a woman, she may be more understanding, but feel just as helpless. Neither woman may understand why this is happening, especially because they are women and "should" feel safer together. A woman may think that because her partner is a woman, she shouldn't have the reactions she might to a man. It is critical to understand that being in a lesbian relationship does not get rid of the SAS. Women learn the Alarm at a young age. It is an automatic primal response not based on one's partner, man or woman. The SAS is non-discriminating. It can't tell the difference between a trusted partner, a man in a parking lot, or a woman. If a woman partner enacts behaviors that are triggering, the Alarm will go off. Our protective Alarms do not have a cognitive part to them. They have become part of our instincts. When the SAS is explained to women partners, they understand because they are also women. Women partners can work more easily with each other because they both know what the other woman experiences.

THE FOUR STEPS OF SEXUAL HEALING

For women who are struggling with sexual issues, there are Four Steps of Sexual Healing that are essential. Through my years of working with women's sexual issues these steps emerged and have held true. Women need to go through these steps in the right order. For healing to take place, you can't skip over a step to the next or to two ahead, although many women, with encouragement from their partners, would like to and try to do just that. The steps are:

1. Establishing safety
2. Setting limits
3. Owning your own female sexuality
4. Expanding your sexuality

In order for a woman to begin to heal, she *must* feel safe. If she does not feel safe, she shuts down. The Sexual Alarm System is a major factor in this step. It is what alerts and protects a woman when she does not feel safe. It tells her to close down and get away. Setting limits involves a woman saying what she likes and doesn't like, being able to say no, and stopping a partner when she is not comfortable to proceed. Owning your own female sexuality means coming in touch with what is right for you as a woman. Many, but not all, women prefer sex that is personal, warm, slow, and caring. They need to begin the sexual experience in ways that work for them, not only for their partners. Women need to discover what their female sexuality is, what their own way is. The exercises in this book are designed to help women find their bodies and open up to physical sensation. This is part of finding themselves and their sexuality. Thus, the exercises are an important way for women to own their own sexuality.

Expanding sexuality involves trying out ways of being sexual that are either new or challenging. For example, it may include viewing erotica or wearing sexy clothing. A woman *cannot* participate meaningfully in these behaviors if she has not done healing in the first three steps. It is very important for women and their partners to understand this. Partners who push a woman to act in experimental ways sexually before she is ready only succeed in triggering the SAS, which shuts the woman down. A male client of mine wanted his girlfriend to dress up for him in high heels and leather mini skirts during sex. He was quite angry that she wouldn't do this. He did not realize that her intense discomfort with this behavior triggered an instinctive reaction over which she did not have control. This is the SAS.

In this book both the couples exercises and adding arousal exercises bring in this Fourth Step of healing for women. They expand a woman's experience into areas that may be challenging and scary. It is crucial that when working with this book, women first experience the exercises that deal with the SAS. These exercises help women with steps one through three.

It is true that there are some women who skip over the first three steps and go right to step four. Usually these are women who have separated themselves in some way from their sexuality and have difficulty with intimate sex. They are a minority.

The Four Steps are crucial for women with sexual dysfunctions and also for women without any particular sexual dysfunctions. Because of the SAS, because of the fear that we as women grow up with about sexuality, we all need healing about sexuality.

SUMMARY

The SAS blares out at women to WATCH OUT. They are prey! They then go through becoming wired, getting triggered, going on high alert, and finally withdrawing and shutting down. Whew! This is stressful and exhausting. And it affects many aspects of women's lives! Most men do not experience the SAS because they are not, in fact, sexual prey. It is difficult for them, therefore, to understand what a woman experiences. Having an intimate relationship with a woman does not get rid of her SAS. It is too well ingrained and automatic. The SAS is an integral part in the Four Steps of Sexual Healing for women. Chapter 2 addresses what triggers the SAS.

Chapter Two

What Triggers the Sexual Alarm System?

Behaviors that tend to trigger the Sexual Alarm System are aggressive, non-personal, objectifying, sudden, non-mutual, forceful actions. But behaviors that may seem intimate, fun, and playful can also trigger the Sexual Alarm. So, can just any behavior trigger the SAS? The key is whether the woman experiences the actions as sexually unsafe.

Chapter 2 discusses two groups of triggers for the SAS. The first group of triggers consists of categories of behaviors related to a woman's experiences. The second group consists of specific physical and visual violations of the Sexual Alarm System.

Here is a short list of behaviors that can trigger the SAS in partnerships:

Being grabbed anywhere, particularly on the breasts, butt, and crotch.
Being approached from behind.
Being held too tightly.
Being held down.
Explicit sex talk.
Being pinched.
Watching porn movies initiated by one's partner.
Direct explicit sexual suggestions ("Let's have sex tonight, honey")
Sloppy wet kisses.
Strong tweaking of the nipples.
Having the clitoris touched too soon.

"But that eliminates all the fun stuff" or "That eliminates everything" a partner might say. What is there left? Some men will say, "Well, sometimes she hates this and other times she likes it. I never know." And others will throw up their hands and say, "Everything has to be perfect and then MAYBE she'll be interested."

Male upbringing in our society promotes the behaviors that trigger the Alarm System. How do men touch? They push, slap, tweak. They touch aggressively. As boys, they wrestle, poke, chase, tackle, jump on, hold, etc. When men talk together about sex, they often talk about "getting laid," "getting off," "jumping bones." Their touch, their talk, their images are direct, explicit, and intense. This is just what turns many women off and sets off their SAS. Women learn that this behavior can be dangerous. If we wanted to create training designed to alienate men and women sexually, we couldn't do a better job.

Devon often tried to pinch Althea. He would get playful and silly. Then would come the pinches and then the bum slaps. Althea asked, explained, and pleaded that she hated the pinches and the slaps. Couldn't he stop and touch her gently? Devon would stop for a few days and then begin all over again.

There certainly are men who approach sexuality in a more soft, gentle, and sensitive way. They are often men who are more aware of what women need, are more gentle people, are more in touch with their bodies, and/or are from other cultures that allow men to be more sensitive and sensual. They may also be from families in which affection and touching are openly expressed by men as well as women. Some men who are comfortable with softer, gentler sexuality resent the categorizing of men as aggressive, insensitive partners. At the same time they often recognize the reality of sexual danger for women.

Isaac knew his partner's body. He would feel her tension, so he would soothe her and let her know it was him. She was safe. Unless she was calm and open, he knew attempting to be sexual would go nowhere. She would stiffen up and close down. He enjoyed taking the time to bring her to him gently.

Women partners tend to trigger the SAS less often because, being women, they initiate more of the kinds of behaviors that another woman would welcome. A woman partner will often initiate the kinds of behaviors that she would like and would make her feel safe. She is more likely to move more slowly and to be emotionally intimate and personal before initiating being sexual. Yet, a woman partner who prefers more aggressive direct sexual contact may well set off her partner's SAS.

TWO GROUPS OF SAS TRIGGERS

Categories of Behaviors Related to a Woman's Experiences

There are several categories of behaviors that trigger the Sexual Alarm. They come from various sources. They may be triggered by events in life, male or female partners, or from a woman's own behavior in the past.

The first category is impersonal, non-mutual, forceful behaviors. This category includes behaviors that women fear experiencing or actually experience out there in the world. They include grabbing, holding down, aggressive sexual talk, and victimizing behavior. Most women have experienced some form of this behavior from a stranger, a date, a boyfriend. Women are reminded of these behaviors regularly on TV, on the news, on the street, in the schools. What about teenage boys forcing girls to give oral sex? What about celebrities, such as Mel Gibson, verbally tearing apart their girlfriends with cutting words?

In therapy, Brianna happened to mention an event in her history that she thought was unimportant because things like it happened to women all the time. Not a big deal. One day in broad daylight, she was parked on a side street in Boston. As she approached her car to leave, she noticed a man standing off to the side, but didn't think much of it. Suddenly, as she unlocked her car and stepped inside, the man jumped into the passenger seat. She screamed bloody murder and scared the man, drawing attention from people around them. The man fled. She counted herself lucky and drove off quickly. By the time she got home and the kids were climbing all over her, she forgot about what happened.

The second category consists of behaviors within a relationship that remind a woman of the above behaviors. These experiences lead the woman to fear behaviors that even so much as suggest that these negative experiences might happen. A woman's husband may think he is playfully grabbing his wife to "invite" her to be sexual, but she may well flinch instinctively to protect herself. Why is she reacting like this? Some of the behaviors in this category are not meant to be hurtful or disrespectful. At the same time it is difficult to see how some other behaviors in this category are not disrespectful. If a woman keeps telling her husband she doesn't like being held down, that it hurts when he rubs her nipple so hard, how does he not understand that she is uncomfortable and that he is scaring her? Perhaps he really doesn't understand because it wouldn't scare him. Perhaps sometimes she likes it. Perhaps he thinks that objecting is what women do. Perhaps he feels he deserves sex anyway.

Later that week when Brianna and her husband Zach were starting to make love, Zach ran his hand between her legs seeking out her genitals. She jolted and pulled away. What? Why? Neither of them understood. Sex stopped. Brianna guessed that she was too wound up from the day at work.

In a group I was running for couples on intimacy and sexuality, at one point I had the women come into the middle of the room and talk openly about what it was like to relate to their male partners sexually. Every woman talked about how her partner's body size was intimidating for her. Note that, indeed, some of the women were not that much different in size than their partners. When the men came in the middle to talk, they were blown away by their partners' reactions. Most had no idea.

The third category consists of behaviors that the woman once enjoyed but now fears. This brings up the major issue of what happens to women as they mature and become part of an intimate relationship. In fact, in their teens and twenties women may enjoy or think they enjoy sexual behaviors from men that later on turn them off. Why is this? When a woman is young and just discovering her sexuality, she is often anxious to prove herself. She wants to be adventurous, daring, and/or attractive to partners. She discovers her own sexual feelings. These experiences override her Alarm System. Her excitement, her sense of her new power, and her arousal override her protectiveness and fear. How do people ride white river rapids and travel to strange worlds? Adrenaline, a need to challenge oneself, newness, wonder. Young women will engage in sexual adventures ignoring the dangers, the embarrassment, and the fear within them. Once in a safe relationship, these fears are not covered up by these stronger urges. Now her inborn SAS is louder than the other factors, which have diminished or disappeared. How embarrassed or ashamed many women feel about how they acted in their teens and twenties! They may scare themselves such that they shut down sexually. The wilder, more open behaviors were not integrated. They were just layered on top of the Alarm and drowned it out. These early experiences may, in fact, end up feeding their fears, especially if they got in hurtful situations in which they were sexually used or abused.

Georgia was the easy one. Boys knew where to go. It was her way of being cool and feeling desired. Sometimes she even enjoyed the sex. But that was years ago. Now in her marriage she felt sexually dead. How Georgia longed for that excitement and yet, how she hated how she had acted. When she thought about how she dressed and how promiscuous she had been, she was mortified. Many sexual experiences she could hardly remember. There were some years when she had a boyfriend and sex was good. Yet, all the time she felt that sex was her ticket to being accepted and her expression of being cool and desirable. Now she could hardly talk about those years, realizing the depth of her insecurity and what she called the "whorishness" of her behavior.

Specific Violations that Trigger the Sexual Alarm System

These violations often fit in the first and/or second categories listed above.

Physical Violations: Touch, Looks, Sounds

There are a variety of physical violations that trigger the SAS.

   1. Aggressive touch from a partner that signals sex is next.   This is the most obvious and common Alarm tripper. Examples of triggering male behavior include:

- Hugs with a pelvic grind and a "ummm" sound
- Grabbing her breasts as soon as he enters the room
- Waving his penis at her as he enters the room (really?)
- Pulling on her clothes to take them off

It can be quite amazing how clueless some male partners can be. They think these behaviors will turn the woman on. Why? Because they turn him on. Because they turn on the women on the porn sites. Because they wish these behaviors turned the woman on. Because they are angry that the woman doesn't respond. Because they want sex with the sexy woman in the magazine, rather than with the woman they married. Fortunately, there are men that do understand that these behaviors don't entice many women. These are men who pay attention to how women respond and to what works for a good sexual experience.

   Some lesbian partners who prefer more aggressive sex or who model themselves on the cultural norm of what it means to be sexual will also initiate aggressive touch that signals sex is next. They are likely to get the same response as male partners get.

   2. Touch that the woman interprets *to mean that her partner wants sex.*

   Most any kind of touch can fit here. The most common are hugs, back rubs, snuggles in bed, and kisses. So, what is a guy supposed to do? He may have no intention of being sexual. It may all be in her mind. Yet, she "knows" what he really wants, so she can feel the sexual energy behind any form of touch. Perhaps she has figured out that he usually does certain types of touch when he wants sex. He probably has not figured this out. He thinks anything he does she interprets as him wanting sex. He's probably right. They are stuck.

   This same dynamic can happen with women partners too. Melanie avoids getting into bed at the same time as Carolina because she fears Carolina's desire to "cuddle" really means she wants to be sexual. Too many times, in Melanie's view, Carolina starts "straying" to strategic parts of her body that are really meant to try to arouse her.

3. Unexpected movements and/or touch.   A husband describes walking into the kitchen one day while his wife was working at the sink. As he walked up behind her, his wife started and flinched without knowing it. She was not aware of her automatic behavior until he told her.

This is an example of how unexpected movements tripped the wife's Alarm. The husband gave this example in therapy after we had discussed the SAS and how it works. Since women don't know when and where sexual danger can come from, they need to be on guard. That guard prepares them for unexpected and uninvited movement.

Unexpected touch particularly can set off the SAS. The guy on the subway whose hand finds its way to a woman's crotch. A husband touching his wife genitally in the middle of the night. The boy in middle school who brushes against a girl's breasts on a dare from a friend. A woman who comes up from behind and puts her arms around her partner's shoulders.

4. Vicarious physical violation.   Examples include witnessing a woman being harassed in person, in the movies, on TV. This happens daily. So a woman can have her SAS triggered anytime? Yes, definitely. Often she doesn't know she's been triggered. She wonders why she isn't interested in sex after the movie is over and she's in bed with her partner. Think about how often there are stories and references in all the different media about women being sexually threatened and/or violated. It is hard to get away from the presence of these scenarios and innuendos. They are in books, newspapers, TV shows, online news stories, and on and on. They are part of jokes and normal conversation. In fact, we are flooded with evidence of women being violated. Women may think these references are about someone else, but they know they are about them, too.

5. A look.   He looks at her breasts. He gives her the once over. She knows he is sizing her up. He is probably imagining having sex with her. The look becomes physical for her. It sends a shock wave through her that is similar to being inappropriately touched. Her Alarm is blaring. She feels violated. Somehow he can just do that—he can just look, stare. She would not dare do that because it would be an invitation to him.

Perhaps he really is just looking at her. She is so used to being aggressively looked at that her SAS goes off anyway. A male client of mine, after hearing the Sexual Alarm System described, decided to test out the premise that women are fearful for their safety around men. He was sitting alone in a hospital cafeteria at a table at the end of an aisle for exiting the cafeteria. To go out people had to walk down the aisle toward him and turn left. The man is a tall, big, and handsome man who his wife describes as a Viking. He decided to try an experiment: to look at each person in the eye as he or she walked out. He wanted to see how the men and the women would react. To his amazement every woman looked away nervously and picked up her pace as she exited. The men on the other hand, looked back at him, some in curiosity and some in greeting. Through this experience he was convinced of the presence of the SAS because he palpably felt the women's fear. Imagine the difference in responses from the men and the women if there had been a woman sitting in his spot doing what he was doing.

6. Sounds. Do women still get catcalled? These days men at construction sites are often more careful. Yet, there are still the whistles, the horn toots, and the "ummms" to navigate most anywhere. When my friend's daughter was sixteen, they were in the car one day and were passed by a truck. As the driver looked down at her daughter, he tooted his horn at her. My friend asked her how she felt about that. She said, "I love it and I hate it." As they discussed it, she described liking being thought attractive and hating that the trucker could just come on to her. What if she had been alone? Then she would have been scared. SCARED! Sounds can cross the Alarm barrier.

Sex talk can trigger the SAS. Do men really believe that saying, "Do you want to have sex tonight" is enticing? And what about more raunchy talk? After a woman is turned on, she may like the raunchy talk. After the SAS is quieted or not even triggered, she may be able to tap into this "sexy" place. Men are confused by this because they don't know about the SAS since they don't experience it. "If she gets turned on by sexy talk part way through sex, why not at the beginning," they will say. Since they don't know about the Alarm, they don't know about the importance of timing for women.

Manny loved it when Sandy "talked dirty" to him. She wanted to give him pleasure and enjoyed seeing him get aroused. So why didn't she get aroused by the "dirty" talk since she seemed to enjoy doing it for him? When we discussed the SAS and how raunchy talk could trigger the woman to shut down, Sandy realized that she was, in fact, turned off by the talking. She did not want to admit it because she was, after all, a sexually liberated woman.

Images

Women are not supposed to be as visual as men. Yet, think of the images that trigger the SAS. Shakira gyrating on the stage seducing men. The porn site that accidently turns up on the computer. The Victoria's Secret catalog that arrives regularly in the mail. These are reminders of what women are supposed to be. But, don't you dare to actually be like that. The wife hopes her husband is not getting turned on by Beyonce on TV and expecting her to writhe for him after dinner . . . at 10 p.m. when she's exhausted, having tried to help little Bethany get to sleep. And . . . he *is* fantasizing just *that* after knowing it is hardly likely. So, women are visual, but it is in the service of their protection. It is not in order to get turned on. The visual images are stimulating for him. For women they are necessary to know about possible danger. They remind women of their inadequacies, their lack of safety. They wish they could be like Shakira. Probably Shakira isn't like Shakira. They may even try in some ways to be like her. Lose weight! Buy that Victoria's Secret underwear! Women want the attention that they don't really want.

Rich and Anya argued about the DVDs he watched. He protested they helped him deal with the lack of sex in their lives. She felt violated and kept thinking of the poor women in the DVDs, imagining their probable histories of abuse. He liked the Victoria's Secret catalogs. She wanted to have them stopped being delivered. They reminded her of what she wasn't and of Rich's disappointment in her body.

SUMMARY

Women can easily become overwhelmed by the number of things that trigger the SAS. It is helpful to understand that there are categories of triggers that make a woman feel unsafe sexually. The two basic types of triggers include 1) three categories of behaviors related to a woman's experiences: impersonal, non-mutual, forceful behaviors; behaviors that remind a woman of these forceful behaviors; and behaviors that the woman once enjoyed and now does not, and 2) specific violations such as unexpected movements and sounds. Chapter 3 explores the physiological background that underlies the SAS in order to understand the fundamental underpinnings of women's sexual experience.

Chapter Three

Physiology

PHYSIOLOGY AND THE SEXUAL ALARM SYSTEM

What role does physiology play in the Sexual Alarm System? Since the Alarm response happens inside women's bodies, it is critical to understand the physiological mechanisms that underlie its existence and functioning. This chapter explores the SAS as an instinct, as a fight/flight response, and as a function of the primal part of the brain, the amygdala. The argument is made that the SAS in not under a woman's control and often not in her awareness. Learning about it brings women relief.

Women's physiology plays a large role in the SAS. There are various ways to understand how women's bodies work. The first way to understand the SAS is to consider it as an instinctive reaction.

Instinct is defined in various ways as illustrated below with definitions from merriam-webster.com:

> 1. A natural or inherent aptitude, impulse or capacity . . .
> 2. a. A largely inheritable and unalterable tendency of an organism to make a complex and specific response to environmental stimuli without involving reason
> b. Behavior that is mediated by reaction below the unconscious level
> (*Merriam-Webster*, 2011)

There is debate about whether an instinct can be modified by learning. Abraham Maslow argued that instincts are not modifiable and human behavior that appears instinctual actually consists of drives. The American Heritage Science Dictionary (*The Free Dictionary*, 2010), however, describes that an instinct, "sometimes involve a degree of interaction with the environment." In fact, it describes instinct in both ways:

An inherited tendency of an organism to behave in a certain way, usually in reaction to its environment and for the purpose of fulfilling a specific need. The development and performance of instinctive behavior does not depend upon the specific details of an individual's *learning* experiences. Instead, instinctive behavior develops in the same way for all individuals of the same species or of the same sex of a species. For example, birds will build the form of nest typical of their species although they may never have seen such a nest being built before. Some butterfly species undertake long migrations to wintering grounds that they have never seen. Behavior in animals often reflects the influence of a combination of instinct and learning. The basic song pattern of many bird species is inherited, but it is often refined by learning from other members of the species. Dogs that naturally seek to gather animals such as sheep or cattle into a group are said to have a herding instinct, but the effective use of this instinct by the dog also requires learning on the dog's part. Instinct, as opposed to *reflex*, is usually used of inherited behavior patterns that are more complex or sometimes involve a degree of interaction with learning processes.

In this book I am using the word instinct to describe behavior that is both inherent and learned. The inherent response in the SAS is our reaction to danger. The learned part involves what we perceive as danger.

Two other elements that come from the American Heritage Science Dictionary discussion of instinct are relevant here: that an instinct is a response that does not involve reason and that it is a reaction that is below the conscious level. Certainly the SAS does not involve reason. It is not reasonable that a woman would flinch when her spouse, who she deeply trusts, initiates sex with her. It is also clear that this is not a conscious reaction. Quite the opposite. The woman is often upset and feels badly about herself for reacting the way she does. If she had control over her reaction, she would be calm, gracious, and loving even if she is not interested in being sexual at that time.

A second way to understand the SAS is as part of the fight/flight response, which is hard wired into human physiology. It is a protective instinct necessary for survival. Other behaviors not part of the fight/flight response can become trained into it if these behaviors become associated with inherent danger to the individual. For example, loud noises can evoke the fight/flight response if someone has lived in a war zone or grown up with an angry, scary parent.

Herbert Benson (2000) in his groundbreaking book *The Relaxation Response* describes the fight/flight response as part of our ability to react to danger and stress. He writes:

When faced with stressful situations, our bodies release hormones—adrenaline and noradrenaline, or epinephrine and norepinephrine—to increase heart rate, breathing rate, blood pressure, metabolic rate and blood flow to the muscles, gearing our bodies either to do battle with an opponent or to flee. (xvii)

This response is an inborn reaction to life threatening stress, ". . . part of our physiologic makeup for perhaps millions of years" (p. 9).

It is innate and helped our ancestors survive. Today it is often elicited inappropriately. We don't often face life-threatening situations, yet we react to stressful situations with this flight fight response.

A third way to understand the SAS comes from the work of Daniel Goleman (2006) in his widely read book *Emotional Intelligence*, in which he goes deeply into the physiology of our response to danger. He describes the amygdala, which consists of two small almond-shaped structures in the brain, as the "storehouse" of "emotional memories" (p. 20). It is the source of our passion and deep emotions. Citing the work of neuroscientist Joseph La-Doux, Goleman describes how the amygdala takes over the thinking part of the brain and, in fact, "hijacks" (p. 17) it. The amygdala scans our experiences for trouble and danger.

> In the brain's architecture, the amygdala is poised something like an alarm company where operators stand ready to send out emergency calls to the fire department, police, and a neighbor whenever a house security system signals trouble. When it sounds an alarm of, say, fear, it sends urgent messages to every major part of the brain: it triggers the secretion of the body's fight-or-flight hormones, mobilizes the centers for movement and activates the cardiovascular system, the muscles and the gut. Other circuits from the amygdala signal the secretion of emergency dollops of the hormone norepinephrine to heighten the reactivity of key areas, including those that make the senses more alert, in effect setting the brain on edge. (p. 16)

These signals prepare the muscles to react and take action. A key part of the process is that the amygdala responds before the neocortex. The amygdala "receive(s) some direct inputs from the senses and start(s) a response *before* they are fully registered by the neocortex" (p. 18). Thus, the amygdala and its emotional system react separately from the neocortex.

Not only do the neuron-chemical alerting systems described above prompt the body to react to stress and danger, they also, "stamp the moment in memory with vividness" (p. 20). Goleman describes the physiological systems that send the memories to the amygdala, which then signals other areas of the brain to strengthen the memories. We then have a special, particularly strong system for emotional memories that is separate from our memory systems for ordinary facts.

However, this neural alarm system for danger is often out of date. In today's life, we don't often face life-threatening situations. Yet, emotional memories can be triggered that send us into the fight/flight response. The signal is rough and can function in a thousandth of a second. The amygdala reacts before knowing the real situation.

We do, in fact, have a manager of emotions, the prefrontal cortex. It assesses reactions before acting and can temper or turn off strong emotions. Goleman (2006) writes:

> One way the prefrontal cortex acts as an efficient manager of emotion-weigh-ing reactions before acting—is by dampening the signal for activation sent out by the amygdala and other limbic centers—something like a parent who stops an impulsive child from grabbing and tells the child to act properly (or wait) for what it wants instead. (p. 26)

This ability to learn is critical to managing our fight/flight responses. It plays a major role is being able to modulate and control the SAS.

Thus, three triggers for the amygdala and the fight/flight response are: dangerous situations, stressful events, and strong emotional memories. The SAS has all three at once. It is based on the underlying fear of a possible dangerous situation, sexual assault. This fear is well trained into every woman even if she is unaware of it. This fear underlies her not going for walks at one in the morning, being extra careful in parking lots at night, noticing any man who is too close or paying her too much attention. Many women have had stressful events that very viscerally tell them of the danger they face. A boyfriend went too far in pushing a woman into unwanted sexual interaction. A friend was raped. A man exposed himself to the woman on the street. These fears and memories are then triggered when a partner, particularly a male partner, does something that startles her sexually such as grabs her breasts or touches her genitals in the middle of the night. Goleman (2006) even refers in an above quote to the amygdala as an "alarm" that signals trouble.

CONTROL

One of the important factors about connecting the SAS with instincts, the fight/flight response, and the amygdala is recognizing that a woman's Alarm System is not under her control. Male partners often believe that women do have control over their pulling away, their fear, and their shutting down sexually, not knowing that they have been triggered. The man becomes angry that the woman is choosing not to respond. Believing that the woman could take in his sexual gestures and get aroused, he feels cheated and controlled or hurt and rejected. The truth is that the woman herself usually would like to not respond in the way she does. Many wish that they could and feel that they should get turned on by their partners' sexual initiations. Women partners may better understand why their partner is pulling away, but still feel rejected and perceive that their partner is choosing to act out.

How is it that this response is not under a woman's control? If she doesn't like how her partner is approaching her, why can't she deflect it or tell him to stop and move on? The reason that she can't just move on is that the SAS stops her in her tracks. She completely shifts gears. She is in an altered state—literally. She can't adapt quickly because the SAS system tells her not to. If you are listening intently to a radio station in your car and suddenly you have to swerve to avoid hitting another car, it's a good thing you can't choose to keep listening to the program. After you have swerved, you can't go quickly back to the program because your adrenaline is pumping. You are in high alert. It takes awhile to calm down. You need to make sure the danger is past. What if a woman and her partner realize that when her SAS goes on alert, she can't just quickly adjust? Then they will have more respect for her process. We know that after a near accident that we need to drive more cautiously and slowly for awhile. Likewise after the SAS has been triggered, a woman needs to slow down or stop, regain a sense of safety, and start over in a non-triggering way. She may need to be held for a few minutes. She may need to cry, breathe deeply, and come back to herself. As I've worked with couples and they learn to honor the SAS and do what is necessary to quiet it and reconnect to each other, they often are able to come back to being sexual and resume or start anew in a way that works for the woman. For example, when Marla would get triggered by something that Mario would do, they learned to stop, talk, and have Mario hold Marla. Then after, she could resume being sexual. At first this was annoying to him, but when Mario came to understand what Marla was experiencing and when he could see how helpful these steps were, he welcomed their interludes. He too became more connected.

Often a woman is not aware that her SAS has gone off and that she is in an altered state. How can this be? In a near accident, we know what is happening. When a ball comes straight at our head and we duck, we know why we are shaken up. Think about other situations when our stress alarm goes off and we don't know it: job pressures, dealing with a difficult child. Years of being accustomed to stressors lead women to experience it as normal. To find a comparable experience, it would need to have these features: 1) the possibility of physical violation, 2) constant reminders of that possibility, 3) minimalization of the experience, and 4) urging of behaviors that bring on the experience, making it seem desirable. The last three features of these experiences push them out of awareness. When reminders are constant, women become habituated to them. Minimizing them dampens women's awareness. Making the negative experiences seem desirable represses the memory of their threatening nature.

RELIEF

When men and women come to understand that the woman's SAS response is not under her control, they usually both feel relieved. How many times I have experienced this in my office as I explain to couples what the SAS is and how it works! The couples learn that the woman's response is not personal to the partner. This is a critical part of grappling with the SAS. In fact men and women come to appreciate that the SAS is there for a reason. It is necessary. What a terrible position a woman would be in without it! It protects her and gives her important information on which to make decisions. Neither of them would want her to walk into a garage late at night and not be vigilant. Neither of them would want her to continue to engage in sex while feeling regularly afraid. Men and women need to learn to work with the SAS, not against it. How relieved men are when they realize that women's response is not their fault and that there is another reason for it! Usually then they want to help and to make the woman's experience different and more positive. In fact, they have often been searching for a reason for the woman's reaction, for something they can do and for something that works. They have often tried many approaches finding no rhyme or reason to explain the woman's responses. They feel frustrated, helpless, and sometimes hopeless.

Understanding the SAS gives them an answer that makes sense. It gives both of them hope for working together rather than at odds with each other. Women partners also feel relieved. Being women also, they are usually quick to understand. They just have not been able to put it together as to why their female partner who is triggered is acting the way she is. Understanding the existence of the SAS can often lead the two women to work together out of a common life experience.

SUMMARY

Women are wired for the SAS because it becomes part of their instinctual fear response, part of their fight/flight physiology. The experiences are stored in the primal part of their brain, the amygdala, a part over which they are not in control and are often unaware of its effect. Whew! "It's not just about me" say many women when they learn how the SAS works. Fortunately, like many of our automatic responses, women can learn how the SAS functions and work with it to control it when they don't want it around. To establish the context for the understanding and treatment of the Sexual Alarm System, Part II explores the background of the SAS, beginning with chapter 4, which presents a brief description of the daunting history of women's sexuality.

II

Background of the Sexual Alarm System

Chapter Four

History of Women's Sexuality

Women and their sexuality have not fared well through history. Women have been considered deranged, inferior, and dangerous. This chapter chronicles views of women's sexuality from ancient times through eras of history into today. It has been and continues to be a rocky ride. This brief history is presented here to help therapists understand the long and complex context of women's disconnection from their sexuality and the development of the SAS.

EARLY HISTORY

From ancient times women and their bodies have suffered from male domination, ridicule, and degradation. They have been confined, mutilated, and stoned. At the basis of this history is male fear of women's sexuality and its perceived power to seduce and destroy them. It was believed that women's sexuality needed to be sharply controlled.

Berman and Berman (2005) write, "From the time of earliest recorded history, about 3,000 BC, women were considered property, valued for reproduction" (p. 21). Any woman who was not a slave was considered first the property of her father and then her husband. A woman who committed adultery was enacting a "crime of trespass against a husband" (p. 21).

Aristotle (381–322 BCE) greatly influenced the concepts of women for many years. He spread his belief that women's bodies were different than and inferior to men's because they were colder than men's bodies. Having less heat "results in her brain being smaller and less developed; in turn, her inferior brain size is the cause of many other defect" (Tuana, 1993, p. 19). A woman, Aristotle believed, was a "misbegotten man" (Weitz, 2010, p. 4).

Classical scholars believed that women had inferior brains and inferior physical constitutions to men. In addition they were characterized by "emotional and moral weakness that could endanger any man who came under their spell" (Weitz, 2010, p. 4). Plato (428/427–348/347 BCE) viewed women's souls as inferior to men's because women were more controlled by their passions and women were less capable in all abilities.

EARLY CHRISTIAN VIEWS

The early Christian church had strongly negative views of women's sexuality. Berman and Berman (2005) write, "The (Christian) church fathers deemed sex unsavory and women a threat to male salvation" (p. 22).

Christianity was strongly affected by the views of Philo, a first-century Jewish philosopher. Philo believed that women were inferior to men for several reasons. The main one was that women were more controlled by sensations and passions, which are inferior to reason. Men, he believed, had superior reasoning powers to women. Augustine (354–430 CE) and Thomas Aquinas (1225–1274 CE), both very influential Christian thinkers, continued these beliefs in their writings. They also viewed women's reproductive responsibility as limiting their rational abilities, giving them a weak temperament.

St. Augustine, a prominent voice in the church, earlier in his life turned against his sexual desires and lust and became celibate. Berman and Berman (2005) describe, "He also wrote that he knew nothing that brought 'the manly mind down from the heights more than a woman's caresses and that joining of bodies'" (p. 22).

At the very basis of Christianity is the story of Eve and Mary. Weitz (2010) writes:

> Christian theologians argued that Eve had caused the fall from divine grace and the expulsion from the Garden of Eden by succumbing when the snake tempted her with the forbidden fruit. This "original sin" had occurred, these theologians argued, because women's nature made them inherently more susceptible to sexual desire and other passions of the flesh, blinding them to reason and morality and making them a constant danger to men's souls. Mary, meanwhile, had avoided this fate only by remaining virginal. (p. 4)

MODERN HISTORY

Martin Luther (1483–1546), the man who began the Reformation, believed that men and women were equal, yet he claimed that men's qualities and abilities were superior to women's. Renaissance thinkers, who also espoused the equality of men and women, were influenced by Aristotle and Aquinas, seeing women as less perfect than men.

Despite some improvement of attitudes toward sexuality and women during the Renaissance and the Protestant Reformation in the sixteenth century, at the beginning of the modern era, women's position legally and socially had changed little.

In America, in Puritan times, sex was considered important in marriage, but attitudes about sex outside of marriage were particularly cruel to women, as evidenced by Nathaniel Hawthorne's (2010) novel *The Scarlett Letter* (Berman & Berman, 2005). Women were chastised for seducing men into sin and punished severely. They remained the property of men (Weitz, 2010).

African American women were, of course, property to be bought and sold, raped for entertainment, and bred to produce more slaves. They were considered animals and sexually depraved.

Change developed in the nineteenth century when in several states women gained the right to "retain property they owned before marriage and any wages they earned outside the home" (Weitz, 2010, p. 6).Women, both white and African American, made further gains in several states in which they were granted the right to vote. The national suffrage movement began. More women entered the work force during the industrial revolution.

In reaction to these changes emerged new attempts to define white middle-class women as frail and incapable of bearing the stress and responsibilities of education and employment (Weitz, 2010). Interestingly, Charles Darwin (1809–1882) contributed to these beliefs, arguing that women were not as evolved as men, were more controlled by their emotions, and had "little energy for either physical or mental development" (Weitz, 2010, p.7) because of their main focus of reproduction. In addition:

> Since Darwin believed that it is generally males who contend for and are selected by females, he concluded that only males would evolve as a result of sexual selection. The female, whose role is to choose but who does not compete, does not evolve and thus, "retains a closer resemblance to the young of her own species." (Tuana, 1993, p. 37)

Along with the view of women as fragile, there was, at this time, a large increase in the gynecological surgeries for women that were both "unnecessary" and "dangerous" (Weitz, 2010, p. 7). For example, removal of the ovaries was performed because it was believed that the ovaries caused mental and physical derangement. In addition there was a considerable focus on women having hysteria as a result of their uteruses and other sex organs.

Craniology was a part of the science of physical anatomy in the mid-nineteenth century. Scientists studied the size and shape of human brains and concluded that because their measures showed women's brain to be smaller than and of inferior shape to men's, women had evolved less and had fewer capabilities.

The nineteenth-century Victorian women were expected to be sexless models of purity and public morality. Women had to suppress their sexuality and husbands were expected to honor their wives by not pushing them sexually. Women considered sex "of limited importance" (Berman & Berman, 2005, p. 27). Prostitution grew as an outlet for men especially as they ventured out into the frontier (Berman & Berman, 2005).

Through the late 1800s a woman's movement against prostitution began. This grew after the Civil War and "included . . . the suffragists Susan B. Anthony and Elizabeth Cady Stanton, who argued that the same standard of morality should apply to both sexes" (Berman & Berman, 2005, p. 26).

At the beginning of the twentieth century, Freud had a major impact on the beliefs and concepts of sexuality. In his writings he opened the door for a broader understanding about the pervasiveness of sexuality as a primal force in our lives. His views of women's sexuality, however, now widely debunked, retained the picture of women as less whole than men with such concepts as penis envy and the vaginal orgasm. "Having posited the incomplete development of the superego in women, Freud argued that this has significant effects on women's character and abilities, including a larger amount of narcissism and vanity, . . . weakened social interests, and a weakened capacity for the sublimation of instincts" (Tuana, 1993, p. 90).

In the 1920s women gained the right to vote in America. Although this was highly significant forward through history, feminist activism largely disappeared at this point. However, important issues such as birth control, the future of marriage, and the commercial exploitation of sexuality were debated during this time. These issues would return in the later part of the 1900s. People developed the view that sexuality would bring erotic enjoyment and was an important part of a happy marriage. However, in the post–World War II era, these views were eclipsed by more conservative values and emphasis on home and family.

In the '20s and '30s a key shift in attitudes developed resulting, in part, from the availability of birth control. Margaret Sanger advocated for the dissemination of various forms of birth control. Her determined fight socially, legally, and medically resulted in making birth control available for many American women. The birth control movement impacted sexuality significantly by separating it from procreation. Sanger was thought to be a radical in her day. Yet urban, working-class women did not benefit greatly from this movement.

A key development in the shift of views about sexuality in general and female sexuality in particular came from the work of Alfred Kinsey in the late '40s and early '50s. The findings of his exhaustive research shocked the culture. His finding that, "women were as capable of orgasm as men" (Berman & Berman, 2005, p. 30) described in his book *Sexual Behavior in the Human Female* (1953) stirred great controversy. Kinsey "labeled it [female orgasm] a 'considerable achievement' attributable to franker attitudes, freer discussion, and the more extensive premarital erotic experience of younger women" (D'Emilio & Freedman, 1997, pp. 268–269).

The 1960s and '70s saw significant changes for women. The development of the birth control pill and its further separation of procreation and sexuality was a leap forward for women to have more control over their bodies and more freedom of sexual expression. A new sexual freedom developed in the '60s, particularly in the youth culture. A permissiveness, evident in the '20s and then in the youth during World War II, reemerged.

In the 1960s came William Masters, a physician, and Virginia Johnson, a behavioral scientist. Their book, *Human Sexual Inadequacy* (1970) outlined four phases of the female and male sexual response cycle based on laboratory findings. This further validated that women can experience sexual pleasure as well as men. It opened up the conversation for women about who they are sexually. Masters and Johnson also refuted Freud's claim of the vaginal orgasm, showing research that "all orgasms for women are clitoral" (Berman & Berman, 2005, p. 31).

The changes in the '60s were certainly not all pervasive. Even within the counter-culture women were abused and men were often the leaders. The changes did not much affect African American and working class women and they had minimal effect on women in such Asian countries as India and Japan (Berman & Berman, 2005).

In the 1980s, the advent of the AIDS epidemic contracted attitudes about sexuality. Condoms, as well as fear, were back. Today people have somewhat adapted to AIDS, as we understand it better and as people with AIDS have access to anti-viral drugs that prolong life (at least in the developed world).

Considering the progress that has been made regarding women's sexuality, Nancy Tuana in 1993 wrote:

Should we breathe a sigh of relief that we live at the end of the twentieth century, when science has progressed so far that we have rejected these erroneous concepts of woman? Such a reaction would be premature . . . belief in woman's inherent inferiority . . . remains a part of the fabric of Western culture. (p.169)

The modern feminist movement has had the goal of equality with men. As the movement shifted and developed various goals, Weitz (2010) describes a backlash that has developed.

This backlash has taken many forms, including (1) increasing pressure on women to control the shape of their bodies, (2) attempts to define premenstrual and postmenopausal women as ill, and (3) the rise of the anti-abortion and "fetal rights" movements (p. 9).

SUMMARY

The brief history given here shows the underpinnings of subjugation and fear of sexuality that have been ingrained in our civilization. Although there has been great progress through the centuries, much remains that keeps women's Sexual Alarm Systems alive and necessary based on the historically deep-seated villainization of women and the strong control of women's sexuality. Chapter 5 looks at the history of sex therapy and compares my book to others on female sexuality.

Chapter Five

History of Sex Therapy and Working with Women's Sexual Issues

Since the 1970s the field of sex therapy has come through infancy, childhood, and adolescence into adulthood. In the 1950s, the depth of understanding of human sexuality and sex therapy treatment that has developed was unimaginable. Now in the twenty-first century we still have a long way to go, especially in our understanding of female sexuality. There are icons in the field that have paved the way for the many directions in which the field has developed. This chapter presents critical work that has laid the foundation and sets the context for the approach to female sexuality in this book. This history can help therapists put the concepts and the therapeutic approach presented here in context.

SEX THERAPY HISTORY

William Masters and Virginia Johnson revolutionized the treatment of sexual dysfunctions with their research on sexual functioning and their behavioral treatment programs. They observed and measured individuals' and couples' sexual responses in the laboratory including, for example, using cameras inside women's vaginas. A key part of their work was the development of the four stages of the sexual response: excitement, plateau, orgasm, and resolution. Their behavioral treatment was based on the belief that breaking a couple's negative cycle of sexual interactions by introducing nonsexual touching and new sexual behavior patterns would create more satisfying sexual experiences that would then generate more sexual interactions. Sensate focus, a program of exercises beginning with nonsexual touch and grad-

33

ually moving to more and more sexual touch and stimulation was a cornerstone of their treatment program for many of the sexual dysfunctions. They
wrote (1970):

> These "exercises" are designed to free sexually dysfunctional individuals from
> inhibitions that deprive them of an opportunity to respond naturally to sensory
> experience. (p. 76)

> The educational process, as initiated in therapy by the sensate "exercises,"
> permits gradual modification of negative reactions to sensory stimuli so that
> learning occurs through return from positive experience. (p. 77)

Helen Singer Kaplan, through her experience working with sexual issues in a
New York City clinic, added another important ingredient to Masters' and
Johnson's four stage model: sexual desire, which she defines in her book
Disorders of Sexual Desire (1979) as follows: "Sexual desire or libido is
experienced as specific sensations which move the individual to seek out, or
become receptive to, sexual experiences" (p. 10). She believed that sexual
desire was a key step in leading to sexual engagement and the subsequent
stages. She also emphasized the importance of underlying psychodynamic
issues for patients for whom behavioral treatments were not sufficient. Thus,
she introduced the significance of treating psychological issues for some sex
therapy patients. She writes (1979):

> while many patients have isolated sexual problems, often the sexual symptom
> appears enmeshed in more extensive psychopathology. . . . Only if such limit-
> ed intervention is not successful are we prepared to work on a deeper level and
> to help the patient to resolve deeper intrapsychic conflicts and transactional
> difficulties which are perpetuating his symptom. (p. 191)

In his book *Constructing the Sexual Crucible* (1991), David Schnarch ques-
tioned some of the premises of the work of Masters and Johnson and Helen
Singer Kaplan, arguing that improved sexual functioning did not necessarily
lead to a better sexual relationship. He argued that Masters and Johnson's
model is, "a purely physiological model without space for phenomenological
experience" (p. 15) and has "the absence of subjective arousal" and "the lack
of consideration of *desire* . . . " (p. 12). He considered these issues to be a
serious limitation of modern sex therapy to date. He emphasized the importance of not just "good enough sex" (p. 62), but "as good as it gets" (p. 68)
sex, bringing in the importance of the erotic element of sexual enjoyment not
just basic sexual functioning. He writes, "sexual-marital therapy must consider the 'disowned' aspects of an individual's eroticism, permitting it to be
recognized, reorganized, validated and cherished" (pp. 51–52). Schnarch in-
corporated a systems approach to sex therapy, emphasizing the importance of

how the dynamics of a couple's relationship affects their sexual relationship. He sees the sexual relationship as a window to the whole relationship. Treatment of sexual issues must involve treatment of larger relationship issues as they are interwoven together.

Rosemary Basson (2007) in her research on women's sexuality questions the desire, excitement, plateau, resolution model for women. She argues that women experience desire quite differently than men. Intimacy is necessary to provide the context for being sexual for women. Her model is circular rather than linear with arousal preceding and overlapping with desire. Intimacy leads to receptivity, to subjective arousal, to arousal and response desire, to sexual satisfaction and back to intimacy. She emphasizes that a woman's experience of subjective arousal is more important than genital arousal. And further she writes not just of desire, but of "responsive" desire because women's desire is in response to the context of the experience. She writes:

> None of this is in keeping with the traditional model of sexual response emerging from the work of William Masters and Virginia Johnson and later explained by Helen Singer Kaplan, whereby desire precedes arousal, orgasm and resolution. (pp. 26–27)

> Rather than waiting for a possibly infrequent innate sexual need or hunger, a woman is particularly dependent on the acceptability of the context of a given possible sexual interaction. This would include the feelings for the partner at the time of the sexual interaction, as well as the larger interpersonal relationship, the woman's mental, psychological, and medical health, and the sexual and cultural contexts. (p. 34)

> A further important evidence-based change to the conceptualization of women's response is recognition of the importance of subjective arousal rather than genital congestion per se. (p. 28)

A simplified version of her model (Basson, 2007) is presented in figure 5.1.

Her work is key in understanding the Sexual Alarm System. Why is intimacy necessary before many women can experience arousal and desire? Precisely because of the SAS. A woman needs to feel safe, cared about, and connected to her partner in order to go around or to work through the SAS. Whereas men are free to experience, and actually encouraged to feel desire continually, women are discouraged from feeling desire. Sexual desire, women are taught, can get you into trouble. Women who show sexual desire are sluts, whores, and prostitutes. Since sexual desire makes a woman vulnerable, she learns that it is more important to be safe. She learns that intimacy needs to precede arousal and desire because then her most vulnerable state is protected. She needs to make sure that she is safe. The Ingredients Exercises and the Progressive Exercises that I present in later chapters are specifically

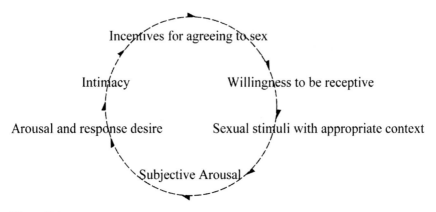

Figure 5.1.

designed to work with this progression of intimacy, subjective arousal, and desire. Safety is continually emphasized. In my program of exercises a woman's body is trained to know how to safely experience many of the dimensions of sexual experience before arousal is added in. A woman needs to know her body in order to allow subjective arousal and desire to connect in. Through these experiences a woman develops a powerful intimacy with herself and her body responses.

TREATING WOMEN'S SEXUAL ISSUES: COMPARISON OF THE SAS AND MY THERAPY APPROACH TO OTHER BOOKS ON WOMEN'S SEXUALITY

There are many books on women's sexuality. There are particular ones that stand out that I love. I love them because they are comprehensive, inclusive, compassionate, and helpful. They speak directly to women in ways that are accessible and meaningful. There are five such books that are gems: Lonnie Barbach's (2000) pioneering *For Yourself*, Andrew Goldstein and Marianne Brandon's (2004) *Reclaiming Desire*, Gina Ogden's (2008) *The Return of Desire*, Wendy Maltz's (1991) *The Sexual Healing Journey*, and Margo Anand's (1989) *The Art of Sexual Ecstasy*. Each of these books addresses the sexual inhibitions women experience and give specific exercises to help women find their sexuality.

One of the first and most influential works was Lonnie Barbach's (2000) *For Yourself*. Barbach's book in the '70s was revolutionary for a number of reasons: 1) it focused on women's sexual experience, 2) it taught women to know and explore their own bodies, and 3) it taught women to masturbate and discover their own orgasms. Imagine women masturbating! Imagine women having orgasms on their own. Many women at that time had never even looked at their vulvas or considered masturbation. Sex was for pleasing men. Barbach's underlying message was that woman's sexual experience was an important part of her life. She needs to know, to understand and to enjoy her sexuality and she can do it BY HERSELF. In fact, by doing so, she can be a better sexual partner. She writes:

> it is essential for a woman to get in touch with her own body and understand her individual requirements for orgasm before she can effectively communicate her needs to a partner. The easiest and most effective means of getting in touch with one's sexual responses is through masturbation. (p. xviii)

Back then we were in awe of the message of this book. These were new and astounding ideas. In *For Each Other* (1983), Barbach continued her work, bringing it into couples' relationships and focusing on what is needed for the woman to fully feel and enjoy her sexuality.

Many more books of all varieties followed Barbach's work. Some of the significant books include Heiman and LoPiccolo's (1988) *Becoming Orgasmic*, and those that are described below.

Goldstein and Brandon (2004) in *Reclaiming Desire* present a comprehensive approach to dealing with issues of low sexual desire in women. Their book looks at issues in four areas of sexual health: physical, emotional, intellectual, and spiritual. In the area of physical sexual health they look at medical issues such as the effects of the hormones testosterone and dopamine. In the emotional arena, they consider blocks to sexuality such as depression, anxiety, and trauma. In the intellectual area, they consider women's thoughts and beliefs about sexuality, parental influences and teachings, and social influences. Discussing spirituality, they encourage women to explore Taoist and Tantric teachings about sexuality in order to learn about sex as a spiritual experience. Particularly helpful in their book is a questionnaire for the reader to fill out to determine in which of the four areas she needs to do the most work. In addition the book has wonderful exercises such as looking at erotic literature, developing sexual fantasies, and nonsexual touch.

Gina Ogden (2008) in her book *The Return of Desire* redefines sexual desire as more than a biological experience. Her ISIS model of desire includes four energies that are essential to women's sexuality: physical, emotional, mental, and spiritual. Her definition of sexual desire says it all:

> Sexual desire goes by many names: attraction, passion, love, energy, libido, and randy, all-consuming lust. It can fill us with wonder. It can lift our hearts, rock our bodies, touch our souls. . . . It also involves the inner woman—our cravings to know and be known. It involves the loves, wishes, dreams, memories, fantasies, and meanings that are ongoing parts of our lives. (p. 3)

Gina brings her wonderful accessible, warm, optimistic energy to her writing. She discusses such important issues as sexual scripts, men, childbirth, lesbianism and bisexuality, abuse and trauma, and sacred union. An important feature of her work is her discussion of the connection of sexuality and spirituality. She describes the sacredness of sex in various ways including a feeling of oneness, waking up to the cosmos, and a connection to the divine.

Wendy Maltz's (1991) book *The Sexual Healing Journey* deals with reclaiming sexuality after a history of sexual abuse. Woman who have been sexually abused have a heightened SAS. On top of the culturally learned fear of sexuality and/or sexual assault, they have experienced specific frightening abuse usually by men or boys. Many of the steps that Maltz describes as needed for sexual healing for survivors of sexual abuse can be used for all women because of the SAS. For example, many non-abused women have internalized negative messages about sexuality and can gain from her suggestions for creating a new meaning for sexuality. Likewise many women in a triggered Alarm state have the automatic self-protective reactions described by Maltz and can gain from her suggestions for working through these reactions. Sexual abuse is a much more extreme version of what women experience with the SAS. The SAS prepares us for the possibility of abuse even though it may not have actually happened. We know it is possible and we are alert and watching out for it. Otherwise we would go out for a walk anywhere at any time of night, or travel freely anywhere in the world, or not worry about the men on the street following us.

Margo Anand's (1989) book *The Art of Sexual Ecstasy* is an amazing book, teaching women to connect their sexuality to spirituality through the Tantric approach blended with Western humanistic psychology. Her book shows women how to transcend sexual fear by creating safe ecstatic experiences that go beyond the world of sexual danger. By connecting sexuality with spirituality, she leads women into a new world, one closed to many of us with Judeo-Christian upbringing. It is a world of the integration of body, mind, and spirit in which sexuality is holy, divine, and glorious. It is the vehicle for union, connection, and praise.

> The path of High Sex helps your body to be free of tensions, your heart to be trusting and open, and your mind to develop such psychic skills as visualization, imagination, and meditation. When this integration has taken place, you are ready for a new, qualitatively higher sexual experience in which physical pleasure becomes a delight of the heart and an ecstasy of the spirit. (p. 3)

I have used and continue to use the approaches in these books. They are essential for women's sexual development. Thank heavens these books and many more are available. Goodness knows we need all we can get.

I add my book to these and wish that you would read them all. My book contributes a specific dimension to the discussion of women's sexuality, a dimension that is touched upon but not covered in other books. The other books are broader whereas mine is more specific and focused. Others often explore more complex experiences such as masturbation, using sexual fantasies, reading erotica, and watching erotic videos. These approaches are immensely helpful, and yet some women are not ready for these experiences. My approach recognizes a fundamental level of distress that all women deal with in being sexual. It goes to a micro-level of bodily reactions that affects all levels of women's sexual functioning. My work breaks down the elements of a woman's sexual experience. It is the approach that is often used in teaching a sport. Movements are broken down into specific sequences. For example, to swim the crawl you need to consider where and when to move your arms and legs, when to roll your body to the side, when and how to breathe, when and how to move your head. Once you know how to do these steps, you don't have to think about it. The movement just flows. Imagine if something made you freeze and shut down before you got into the water to swim. Imagine this happening over and over again. Eventually you would be blocked, you would forget, you wouldn't be able to move well. Or what if you never did learn the crawl because swimming seemed forbidden and dangerous? This book addresses how women can learn to "swim" in such a way as to move beyond their fears and learn the movements they need to be sexual.

It is very important for each individual woman to know and make a list of what triggers her Alarm. Many of the behaviors that trigger her may be common to women in general. For each woman there will also be specific triggering behaviors based on the woman's upbringing and history. If a woman has had specific violating and/or abusive sexual experiences, she will have a stronger SAS. Looking at the experiences she had will give information about the triggers that trip her Alarm. For example, one woman's father used to give her inappropriate wet kisses on the lips. As a result, kissing, other than soft dry kisses, triggered her SAS in a powerful way. A woman's partner may be able to contribute to the list from his/her experience of her. Once a woman knows her triggers, she needs to honor these triggers and recognize that they exist separately from her partner. She brings her own SAS history to the relationship. Together partners need to work on handling the SAS.

My work follows in the tradition of behavioral sex therapy established by Masters and Johnson. I give exercises to improve the possibility of a satisfying sexual experience for women, and for men. I build on the work of Helen Singer Kaplan and Rosemary Basson. In addition, I follow in the tradition of books to help women reclaim their sexuality, to define their sexuality as their own, and to expand the possibilities of their sexual experience. With all the obstacles there are for women, it is hard to imagine that there could be too many quality books to help women find their sexuality.

Sensate focus exercises have been considered the staple of sex therapy behavioral exercises for couples. They are often the place that therapists start the treatment of sexual issues. Yet, for many women sensate focus exercises are too much too fast. One couple I saw had been assigned the beginning sensate focus exercise by a previous therapist. They made no progress and the exercise froze them in their tracks. This was a couple that had not had sex and had not seen each other nude in fifteen years. The woman particularly had no sexual feelings or desires. Imagine this couple going home to try nude nonsexual touching. I started them with an exercise of sitting on the couch holding hands while watching TV. Many of us who practice sex therapy have learned that you need to begin with what the individual or couple can handle. The exercises in this book are designed to help women discover their bodies in a safe and fundamental way that does not trigger their Sexual Alarm System. They progress in a way that allows them to build experience and confidence alone and with their partner. This is critical for them to move forward.

SUMMARY

Masters and Johnson, Helen Singer Kaplan. They built the ballpark. And many have come to further develop the work of sex therapy. David Schnarch vastly expanded the park, making us look at the whole context of the sexual relationship. In the field of women's sexuality there is Lonnie Barbach and now Rosemary Basson plus many more who have spoken up about the particular issues, oppressions, and needs that women experience sexually. Rosemary Basson's work is particularly important for the concepts and exercises in this book. This chapter has paid tribute to and summarized some of the ground breakers in the fields of sex therapy and women's sexuality. It is in this context that my work on the SAS has unfolded. Chapter 6 shows the continued struggle for women to feel safe in their sexuality by looking at girls' sexual development and today's oversexualization of girls and women.

Chapter Six

Sexual Development of Girls and the Sexual Alarm System

As you look around you at girls today, as you read the newspapers and magazines about girls, what is most striking? The increased sexualization of childhood, especially of girls, and the differences in expectations for girls and boys around sexuality. There is a poster in a local hair salon near me showing a young preschool girl wearing fishnet stockings, sunglasses, lipstick, and a punk sexy hairdo. It is supposed to be cute. It is, in fact, disturbing. This chapter exposes the prevalence of sexual pressures on girls, pressure that comes from today's culture of sexualization reaching to younger and younger ages. As therapists helping women, it is crucial that we grapple with these pressures and their devastating effects. The chapter also brings in the psychology of women and girls.

GIRLS' SEXUAL DEVELOPMENT

It starts very early. Beginning in infancy, gender roles are cast. Girls are soft and boys are tough. Girls are stroked and cooed while boys are boxed and tough talked. Boys wear blue and red and are already members of Red Sox Nation or the NFL. A mother trying to find an outfit with airplanes on it for her infant daughter could only find boys' clothes. We know that boys are expected to be more physical and girls more verbal. Laura Berk (2006) reports numerous socialized gender differences between boys and girls. For example,

> Parents give their sons toys that stress action and competition . . . , while giving their daughters toys that emphasize nurturance, cooperation and physical attractiveness. . . . Parents also actively reinforce independence in boys and closeness and dependence in girls. (p. 531)

By toddlerhood little girls are thoroughly feminized. They are cautioned whereas boys are encouraged. Boys take more risks and are more aggressive. Some say this is biological and hormonal. Yet, how can we separate the biological from all the rampant conditioning that pushes boys to be more active and physical and girls to be pretty and protected? There is no double blind study in which we can truly expose boys and girls to the identical conditioning and see what differences may then result. The messages about the Sexual Alarm System start early and are well underway by toddlerhood. As an example, how many girls have boy babysitters? Why is that? It was at age three that my daughter heard the man in the grocery store say, "You better watch out for her when she grows up." She probably didn't understand the words, but how could she not have felt his admonishing tone of danger? We see the beginning of the sexualization of girls at this stage and even earlier. Therapists certainly hear stories of women clients whose sexual abuse began at this tender age. It is horrifying!

By elementary school the sexualization of girls is frightfully prevalent. What is sexualization? It is the imposing of sexual attitudes, behaviors, and expectations on a child beyond the child's capacity to understand, to integrate, and to react appropriately. Sharna Olfman (2009) in her book *The Sexualization of Childhood* defines sexualization as

> *derailed* psychosexual and gender development as a consequence of cultural values, beliefs, norms, and practices that:
>
> - teach girls that their primary worth is in their ability to be sexual objects for male pleasure
> - teach boys that sex and violence are conjoined and that girls and women should be valued primarily for their ability to give them sexual pleasure
> - isolate sexuality from personhood and the capacity for emotionally intimate and committed relationships
> - treat children as if they are sexually mature because of the outward trappings of wardrobe, makeup, or precocious puberty
> - allow corporations to use materials or methods of production that release endocrine-disrupting chemicals into the environment, contributing to early puberty (p. 2)

Diane Levin (2009) in her chapter, "So Sexy, So Soon: The Sexualization of Childhood" in Olfman's book gives the following examples of the sexualization of girls:

A seven-year-old asking her mother, "What's a blow job?"

Beauty pageants for young girls like the one in which JonBenet Ramsey participated

Sexualized toys such as the Bratz dolls

Increased sexualization even of Disney characters. Pocahontas has more cleavage, wears fewer clothes and is much sexier than Cinderella

Levin writes, "Girls are taught that they should have skinny bodies and that they need to be consumers of clothing, makeup, and accessories in order to look 'pretty,' 'grown-up,' and 'sexy'" (p. 79). At this stage children are concrete thinkers able to think of just one thing at a time. They don't yet understand the motivation, intentions, and feelings that underlie their sexualized behaviors. Thus, they focus on thinness or sexiness without the understanding of what they mean or how they are related to values, sense of self, and relationships. Levin argues that what we as adults need to be doing at this age for children is laying the foundation for healthy sexual relationships by giving models of caring relationships. Instead we are teaching girls to aspire to unattainable models of attractiveness, thus inspiring self-deprecation and self-hate. Margo Maine (2009) in her chapter "Something's Happening Here: Sexual Objectification, Body Image Distress and Eating Disorders" in Olfman's book writes, "The single-best predictor of risk for developing an eating disorder is being born female" (p. 64). She further explains:

> In a highly charged sexual environment, girls feel pressured to look "sexy" but also fear sexual vulnerability and violence. Girls' bodies become simultaneously "hot commodities" and danger zones. Eating disorders symptoms, such as excessive dieting, exercise abuse, and purging, can become a safety net yet lead to their own risks with high costs to the physical, emotional, cognitive, social and spiritual health of suffering females and their loved ones. (p. 64)

Girls in elementary school are already viewed by men as desirable sexual objects. Parents have to thwart girls' desires for independence and freedom by making sure that they are rarely alone out in the world where they could be abused or kidnapped. Even teachers add to girls' vulnerability by treating boys and girls differently. Berk (2006) writes, "teachers interrupt girls more than boys during conversation, thereby promoting boys' social dominance and girls' passivity" (p. 534).

The distinction between preteens and teens is rapidly diminishing, especially as the age of sexual development lowers. Girls are having their periods and developing breasts at an increasingly younger age. "Tweens" are more and more sexualized in appearance, in advertising, and in expectations of their behaviors. Preteens look to their teenage siblings and neighbors plus increasingly their teen idols in the media and emulate their behavior. Not that this is new. Yet, what they see and copy now are increasingly sexualized and provocative images of who they should be. The move to kill sex education at this vital age leaves preteens (and teens) less knowledgeable and more vulnerable to unrealistic expectations and exploitation.

Adolescents now face the same issues as grown women: fear of victimization and sexual violence, pressure to be sexy without being sexual, and objectification and depersonalization. Teens are especially vulnerable to the effects of the media and to peer pressure to conform.

Jean Kilbourne in her DVD *Killing Us Softly 3* (2002) points out a number of particularly frightening characteristics of how women are portrayed in the media:

1. Women's bodies are increasingly unreal. The images of women are altered in such a way the women don't resemble how any real person actually looks. Few women have the body type of models and most models who have large breasts have had breast enhancement surgery. In addition, "boob jobs" cut off significant sensation in women's breasts, making them pure objects not capable of subjective pleasure for the women.
2. Women are often shown in passive postures as opposed to men who are shown as active and strong. Worse, some advertising images show women being victimized and treated violently, for example, having their hair being pulled, being stepped on, sitting open-legged with bottles positioned to enter their vaginas.
3. Women are shown being silenced in different ways including with their own hands over their mouths.
4. Black women are shown as animals and as creatures complete with animal headdresses and plumes.
5. Women's body parts are highlighted and sexualized in an objectified way.
6. Increasingly teens are portrayed in hypersexualized images.

This is what we teach girls. It is frightening that these are the models girls emulate. How can we take away sex education at the same time that we let kids see more and more sexualized TV? How can we serve preteens and teens Miley Cyrus and Britney Spears at the same time that we preach abstinence? Bristol Palin on "Dancing with the Stars" in 2010 said it well when she was caught off-stage wondering how she can be out there preaching abstinence while she is also onstage in her underwear dancing sexily? Kilbourne now has *Killing Us Softly 4* (2010) which reiterates and updates these themes plus shows how the images of women are photoshopped and manipulated such that the images we see are not any real person.

Some of the messages for preteens and teens have not changed:

"Boys are after one thing. Be careful."

"Don't go out in the dark."

"Be a good girl."

And some have:

"Comply with what boys want to be popular."

"Don't be a virgin too long."

"Giving boys oral sex is being cool."

Adolescent girls are caught in an impossible bind. We expect them to be increasingly sexy while we don't acknowledge that they are sexual. We do not acknowledge that they may have sexual feelings and interests of their own. Deborah Tolman (2002) in her book *Dilemmas of Desire* writes of this issue:

> Despite the incessant flow of sexual images and relationship advice, girls do not get many positive messages about their sexuality. They are barraged with an ever more confusing and contradictory set of guidelines for how they should manage their developing sexuality: don't be a prude but don't be a slut; have (or fake) orgasms to ensure that your boyfriend is not made to feel inadequate, if you want to keep him. Ultimately, though subtly, the media continue to represent the belief that adolescent girls should be sexy for boys and not have their *own* sexual desires. . . . And so the conundrum: while *sexualized images* of adolescent girls are omnipresent, *their* sexual feelings are rarely if ever portrayed. (pp.7–8)

Tolman further writes about how the social construction of femininity results in girls being disconnected from their bodies. Her study of teenage accounts of feeling sexual desire shows a range of experiences, many of them filled with disembodiment, confusion, and/or rebellion against the norms of repressing female desire.

PSYCHOLOGY OF GIRLS AND WOMEN

Writing in 1976, Jean Baker Miller, a psychiatrist, was one of the first writers to argue for a unique psychology for women. In her book *Toward a New Psychology of Women, 2nd ed.* (1986) she challenged the belief that women were inherently less than men by looking at women's so-called "weaknesses" as also their strengths. She showed how women's qualities such as serving others, vulnerability, strong affiliation with others, ability to cooperate, and creativity were sources of great strength. Men, in fact, suffer from a lack of ability to connect, having been taught to override the need for affiliation with the drive for autonomy. As a result, our culture, being dominated by male values, is plagued by alienation and isolation. She urges women to find their authentic selves by discovering their own needs and desires. A woman's real self needs to be developed personally, sexually, and in relation to the world.

Baker writes of the importance of a woman finding her sexual authenticity, which involves "accepting her own sexuality and allowing herself sexual pleasure" (p. 107). This will "allow her to tap all of her suppressed energies and direct them toward her goals" (p. 107). There is a risk of women displeasing others in this journey to find their true selves. Yet, women discovering themselves and speaking up for themselves is essential to change the balance of power from male domination to gender equality. Miller's work was the basis of the psychology of women which has developed over the last several decades, particularly from the Wellesley Centers for Women.

Carol Gilligan has also contributed significantly to the psychology of women. She worked at Harvard University with Lawrence Kohlberg on moral development. Because Kohlberg's work was developed from males, Gilligan broke with Kohlberg and developed her own research and theory about women's moral development. In her book *In a Different Voice* (1982) she describes that women's moral development is not marked by autonomy as the highest level but by a morality that is relational. That is, women consider others' feelings and needs in making moral choices and decisions. Whereas men are more individualistic, women are more concerned about personal relationships and community. This description of women fits with Rosemary Basson's research that finds that women's sexuality and sexual desire is contingent on intimacy in a relationship. Gilligan's as well as Basson's work support my formulation of the SAS and what women need to deal with the SAS: safety, intimacy, and support.

In addition to her work describing how women's moral development is different than men's and that women are more relationship oriented that autonomy oriented, Carol Gilligan did seminal work on the development of girls into adolescents. Through interviews with a group of girls from a girls' school she and her co-researchers uncovered a dramatic change in girls as they entered adolescence. Prior to adolescence she found that girls were strong-minded, and able to speak of their feelings, conflicts, and opinions. She and coauthor Lyn Mikel Brown in their book *Meeting at the Crossroads: Women's Psychology and Girl's Development* (1992) write:

> Listening to seven- and eight-, ten- and eleven-year-old girls, we . . . have heard in girls' voices clear evidence of strength, courage, and a healthy resistance to losing voice and relationship . . . the young girls we have been listening to are striking as they speak freely of feeling angry, of fighting or open conflict in relationships, and take difference and disagreement for granted in daily life. (pp. 3–4)

Yet, as the girls became adolescents, they lost this clarity and strength and went through a disconnection from themselves.

> Over the years of our study, even as they became more sophisticated cogni-
> tively and emotionally, young girls who had been outspoken and coura-
> geous . . . became increasingly reluctant to say what they were feeling and
> thinking or to speak from their experience about what they knew . . . not
> speaking turned into not knowing . . . as the process of dissociation itself was
> forgotten. (p. 217)

This resulted in a separation from their psyches and their bodies. They became focused on what other people wanted of them and on an idealized
image of who they should be. Frighteningly, they began to ignore and not
know signs of emotional and physical abuse. They disappeared and thus
became very vulnerable.

Gilligan writes that it is crucial that women become involved with girls at
this transition in their lives in order to help them stay in touch with who they
are. She has been involved in programs promoting the development of girls'
strengths and self-knowledge. She has been recognized with a number of
prestigious awards for her important work.

Gilligan's work is important for contributing to the understanding of how
girls lose their confidence at the time that they are developing sexually. This
change further shows the need for girls to have a strong Sexual Alarm System. Already well established, the SAS now has a more powerful job to do to
protect adolescent girls from the dangers that have become stronger and that
the girls are ignoring.

SUMMARY

Thus, girls arrive into adulthood ingrained with the fear of sexuality, fully
aware of the possible sexual danger to them, and full of shame about their
real bodies. Increasingly girls are oversexualized, leading them to detach
from their bodies. The Sexual Alarm System is well internalized beginning in
girls' early years and thoroughly reinforced as girls grow up. Every op-
pressed group learns strategies and skills to protect themselves from harm,
subjugation, violence, and a damaged sense of who they are. The SAS is a
prime tool for women. In fact, how would women survive without it? Would
we wish for women to go out into the night and not know how to protect
themselves? Would we wish for women to not be able to read the signals of
sexual danger? Certainly not! Yet, would we wish for them that they not
enjoy their sexuality, that they not be able to fully participate in a loving
sexual relationship, that they feel lack of confidence in their sexual feelings?
That is the conundrum. With one comes the other. Chapter 7 looks at yet
more sources of women's fear of their sexuality and detachment from their
bodies.

Chapter Seven

Women's Fear of Sexuality: Additional Issues

The case has been clearly made that women have been taught to fear their sexuality and that this fear manifests into the Sexual Alarm System for protection. Christianity, science, and the media have contributed and do contribute to this fear. Women have been considered deranged, dangerous, inferior, animalistic, and much else because of their sexuality. There are yet more reasons women fear their sexuality, reasons related to those already given. These include family history, motherhood, medical issues, lesbianism and bisexuality, and multi-cultural views of women's sexuality. This chapter will explore these issues to give yet a fuller context for women's struggle with their sexuality and the effects of their SAS. These summaries cannot do justice to the knowledge and research available to therapists in each area. I urge therapists to read more extensively in those areas in which they are less knowledgeable.

FAMILY HISTORY

Critical to a woman's development of her sexuality is the atmosphere about sexuality in her home. The predominant stories are these: sex doesn't exist, sex is bad, and/or sex is used abusively. "Sex doesn't exist" usually means there is no mention of it nor any evidence of its existence. Parents do not demonstrate any sexual interest in each other and nothing is taught to the children about sexuality. Of course, it is nearly impossible to create a household in which sex doesn't exist, so there are leaks of various types: parents heard making strange noises, pornography found on Dad's computer, something weird about Uncle Joe, etc. For girls in particular the "sex doesn't exist" model is stronger than for boys. No names are given for the sexual parts of girls' bodies. The beginning of menstruation is not discussed. Perhaps a pad is handed to the daughter when she tells mom she is bleeding. Girls are supposed to be "good." Girls are not supposed to know.

The "sex is bad" model is often religiously based. In many religions, sex is highly controlled. In fact, religions get a great deal of power from their ability to control such a strong force of human nature. Women particularly are repressed in many modern world religions. Branches of Judaism, Christianity, and Islam as well as other religions give women fewer privileges, more constraints, and less freedom. We have seen how women fared in early Christianity. The message continues to be that women's sexuality is dangerous and must be controlled and protected. Many women suffer from upbringing that lets them know that an essential part of who they are is wrong, humiliating, and treacherous. Through the family's religious beliefs, this can take the form of disapproval, shaming, and punishment for any behavior that appears to be sexual.

Many women describe the negative messages they received from their mothers about their sexuality. Their mothers are sexual beings? They remember their mother's embarrassment about all things sexual. Or they remember "the talk," the one awkward time mothers tried to impart some knowledge about sexuality. But the main message was, "It is not something you will enjoy and you do it for your husband." Nancy Friday (1977) in her widely read and deeply probing book, *My Mother Myself* writes:

> What she (the mother) does know is that for a little girl—as opposed to a little boy—sex is a danger. It must be denied, suppressed. Her daughter will not be raised a sexy hussy, but "a lady." No erotic stimuli must intrude into the little girl's consciousness, no dirty jokes, no daring clothes, no indication that the mother's own body responds sexually. If mother doesn't mention it or think about it or respond to anything herself, it will go away. In order to keep the child's attention from turning to the anxious-making topic of sex, the mother goes the final step and desexualizes herself. (p. 21)

In too many households her words still apply today, despite the saturation of sex into our culture. When it comes to daughters, mothers who have repressed themselves don't know what to do.

In 1991, when Demi Moore appeared on the cover of *Vanity Fair* (August, 1991) nude and pregnant, she was widely condemned for degrading motherhood by sexualizing it. She broke the taboo that mothers are not sexual beings and their bodies should be hidden. Years earlier I had seen pregnant women in Bermuda in bikinis on the beach quite comfortable showing their bellies and enjoying their bodies. Other cultures handle sexual issues differently. Some women hailed Demi Moore's courage and took her as an example that women are sensual beings at all stages of life. Motherhood doesn't end it. Yet, for many women sexuality and motherhood are incompatible. How many obstetricians talk with their pregnant mothers about their sexual life post delivery? Perhaps more do now. Mothers are virginal. Mothers are totally preoccupied by mothering. There isn't time for sexuality. There is the reality of how totally consuming motherhood is. And there is the lack of support for women to rediscover their sexual selves as mothers.

Girls' relationships with their fathers regarding sexuality often fall into three categories: nonexistent, complicated, or unsafe. What does a father do when his daughter begins to develop? He often can't handle it so he distances himself, no longer hugging his daughter or being affectionate. On the opposite end of the spectrum are fathers who violate daughter's boundaries by ogling them in bikinis, kissing them too long, confiding to them about their affair with another woman, or outright sexually abusing them. In between are any number of complex mixes of distance, emotional dependence, and triangulation with mother.

Victoria Secunda (1992) in her book *Women and Their Fathers* writes of the father's role in a daughter's life. She states, "Many fathers are not just uninvolved; what's striking is that their daughters are simply not a priority" (p. 33). Girls end up with "father hunger" (p. 33), which is especially strong for daughters whose fathers are not around through divorce, death, or incapacity to handle a daughter. A daughter's sexuality is especially problematic. "But when the daughter hits adolescence, her gender now blatantly obvious, Daddy may again beat a hasty emotional retreat" (Secunda, p.11). She goes on to describe how fathers treat daughters differently than sons: fostering dependency, treating them as fragile, denying their sexuality. Daughters learn to ignore and fear their sexuality from their father's denial and confusion. In fact, fathers feel a natural attraction to their daughters, which alarms them and often chases them away or prompts them to repress their daughters.

Siblings often play an important role in a child's sexual development. Older siblings lead the way and are often the source of information about sexuality, for better or worse. Younger siblings tend to be more influenced by older ones than vice versa unless they are close in age. Often siblings develop in reaction to other siblings (Mersky Leder, 1991). If the older sibling is rebellious and sexual, the younger may be more obedient and conservative. Siblings tend to pass on the messages from the current cultural mores about sexual behavior. Girls may fare best when they have an older sister who informs them, warns them, and guides them.

Particular family histories also can greatly influence a woman's sexuality. Parental alcoholism and the behavioral issues that result can lead to a fear of being out of control. Divorce and remarriage can raise issues about parents being sexual in unexpected and upsetting ways. Since daughters are often more emotionally tuned into family dynamics than are sons, they may feel the effects of such issues, particularly those that involve sexuality.

How does this relate to the SAS? In many ways the family becomes a vehicle for training the SAS in the daughter. The family is the carrier of the messages from the larger society. How often do parents thoughtfully and carefully teach their children not only about the plumbing of sexuality, but also about how to form healthy emotional sexual relationships? How often do parents teach their children, particularly daughters, about how their bodies can have fulfilling sexual experiences? Most often daughters learn to fear sexuality. Mothers and fathers know the dangers for girls sexually. They usually don't know about sexual empowerment for women. So they watch how their daughters, but not their sons, dress. They make sure their daughters are home at a decent hour. They worry about their daughter's reputation. They worry about pregnancy and rape. They keep quiet or make loaded comments when they need to communicate.

How does this parental denial and repression of their daughter's sexuality work in an age of oversexualization of girls? Parents often feel out of control against the impact of the media, the culture, and peer pressure. They don't know what to do. They see their girls getting caught up in the exploitation and they feel unequipped to deal with it, so they don't. Parents have become increasingly afraid to set limits. At the same time, they don't know how to teach and guide their children about what they are hearing and seeing. We have then, a generation of overly exposed girls with less protection. The Sexual Alarm System is ever more present and ever more ignored . . . until the girl becomes older and tries to engage in intimate relationships. She then carries even more baggage that gets in her way.

At the same time, there are hopefully more parents today who are active in their daughters' sexual education and who teach positive messages about physical and emotional development. When I ask my graduate students how many of them came from homes in which sexuality was dealt with in an healthy and appropriate way, maybe a third of the class now raises their hands. Twenty-five years ago I was lucky to get one or two hands. More parents have had some sex education than did their parents, who usually had none. Christiane Northrup (2005) writes movingly of her own role in channeling one of her adolescent daughter's physical and emotional energy:

> As a mother, I feel like a gardener who has been fertilizing and aerating this soil for years. Now something strong is coming through this child that is far bigger than I am. But I must continue to water and feed this force so that it can grow straight and tall—and not bend and break before it has even had a chance to develop bark on the tender areas. (p. 458)

Let us hope that there are more parents who see their role to be as similarly empowering of their daughter's sexuality and development. This is what is needed to deal with the SAS.

MEDICAL ISSUES

The medical aspects of sexual health are often more involved for girls and women than for boys and men. Girls menstruate. They have PMS. They develop breasts. Women bear children. Women get yeast infections, have vaginal pain, and are more symptomatic with STDs such as HPV. Girls make a pilgrimage to their first gynecological visit and have a speculum put into their vaginas. They have hymens to be preserved or broken. Compared to these issues, boys' sexual health is more simple. Not that there aren't diffi-cult issues for boys also. But medically they are fewer. How many adolescent boys go off to a urologist? So what is the significance of these experiences for women? Often going through them is humiliating, upsetting, and scary. Many girls describe being flustered, frightened, and/or embarrassed when they first menstruate. Do they even know what is happening? Some have told me they thought they were bleeding to death. Can they tell anyone?

One of my clients described being tested for infrequent menstruation as a teen. Her vagina was visited by a team of young doctors peering at her and speculating as to what was wrong. Girls and young women who go through medical issues may well learn that their bodies give them problems; that their sexual parts are mysterious, unpredictable and painful; that doctors don't know how to handle them; and that in the end they wish their bodies and sexuality would just go away. Certainly these experiences reinforce the SAS. They may literally make them scared of being touched. Elizabeth Stewart (2005) in her groundbreaking book *The V Book: A Doctor's Guide to Complete Vulvovaginal Health* writes:

> the vulva and the vagina are hidden "down there" below layers of pants, pantyhose, underwear, and panty liners. The Vs have been kept out of sight metaphorically too, by myths, cultural taboos, and for a long time, a lack of medical interest . . . we often associate these parts with the realm of the untouchable or dirty.. Or we don't think about them at all until a problem crops up, and then we aren't sure what to do about it. (p. xx)

Books like hers and Berman and Berman's (2005) are making medical infor-mation about sexuality and the body more available for women. Hopefully this is changing how women experience their bodies and how they deal with medical issues regarding sexuality.

LESBIANISM AND BISEXUALITY

One of my clients described feeling attracted to girls in middle school. After her first time kissing a girl, she went home and threw up. What a flood of tears poured out as she remembered the shame she experienced. On top of all the issues girls must face in becoming sexual, discovering that you are attracted to other girls adds a whole other complicated and often frightening layer. Savin-Williams (1997) writes, "A feeling of being alone, deserted, or in a vacuum characterizes the childhood of many youths who eventually will identify as bisexual, gay, or lesbian. Such youths feel that they belong nowhere and that they have no base of support" (p.158).

We know that gay teens' suicide rate is higher than that of heterosexual teens. "Gay, lesbian, and bisexual youths are also at high risk for suicide, making attempts at a rate three times higher than other adolescents" (Berk, 2006, p. 458). We know that there is verbal and physical taunting and harassing that gay teens endure. The negative messages that girls receive about lesbian sexuality are intense. It is wrong, it is unmentionable, and it is perverted. "Not my daughter, please God." Savin-Williams (1997) writes, "the revelation of a youth's sexual orientation (as bisexual, lesbian, or gay) frequently produces a family crisis . . . commonly, parents subject a youth to verbal castigations, anguished warnings, and denials and invalidations of the youth's feelings . . ." (p. 171).

We live in a day and age in which girls' attraction to girls is becoming more acceptable . . . that is, to some. In the media we see more gays and lesbians, such as Ellen DeGeneres. Gay marriage has become legal in several states. "Don't Ask, Don't Tell" has been repealed. We also live in a time in which there is a growing backlash to this acceptance. The news reports regular anti-gay incidents and diatribes. Bisexual youth have specific issues of their own and are often rejected by both straight and gay teens (Ochs & Rowley, 2005). All of this contributes another layer of negativity about one's sexuality to a lesbian or bisexual girl and woman. It adds another level of self-protection to their SAS.

At the same time relating sexually to another woman can be affirming of one's female sexuality (Stendhal, 2003). Another woman may feel safer. She will probably better understand her partner's fears. She mirrors back familiarity and similarity physically and sexually. And she too has an SAS.

MULTICULTURAL VIEWS OF WOMEN'S SEXUALITY

I would like to find a culture in today's world in which women are sexually empowered and do not need an SAS. I have yet to find such a culture. My graduate students in Human Sexuality picked cultures all over the world to research about sexuality. We were excited in the beginning and depressed at the end after the reports were in. The students used the online Continuum Complete Comprehensive International Encyclopedia (2008) available on the Kinsey Institute website (http://www.kinseyinstitute.org/ccies/). This encyclopedia gives comprehensive research information on numerous aspects of sexuality in many countries. Culture after culture from Brazil to India are filled with forms of oppression of women's sexuality. Harsh rules and procedures are used to control and repress women's sexual expression. Here is a quote from the entry on India:

> Despite new currents, very often in Indian culture a woman's body is not seen as an object of pride or pleasure, but as something that is made impure every day, an abode of sinfulness. Thus, a muted yet extremely powerful theme can be found in Hindu marriages: "the cultural unease, indeed, the fear of woman as woman." (*The Continuum Complete International Encyclopedia of Sexuality,* 2011)

And from Brazil:

> Brazil being a typically Latin and machismo society, males enjoy a superior, almost demigod status. This is reinforced by the economic dependence of women. Only about 18 percent of the women are employed outside the home; the majority devote their time to caring for their house and children . . . she does everything for the children but gives less to the husband . . . criminal violence and the preservation of health are preoccupations more important than sexual pleasure or the fear of getting older. (*The Continuum Complete International Encyclopedia of Sexuality,* 2011)

Sonya Grant Arreola (2005) writes about Latina child sexuality. In looking at the role of the father with his daughter, she describes that Latino fathers are very concerned with "protecting their daughters from a sexually dangerous society" (p. 50). The examples of women's sexual struggles throughout the world go on and on.

Lynn Nottage's (2010) play *Ruined* is a riveting portrayal of rape as a weapon of war in the Belgian Congo. The play is at times harrowing in its picture of the brutality done to women. Nottage brings to light a phenomenon that occurs all too commonly as part of war around the world. What place does sexual violation of women have in wartime?

It appears that oppression of women's sexuality in fairly universal. With this oppression comes the SAS. Is it different anywhere—perhaps in Sweden or in Tahiti? Although clearly women are sexually safer in some countries more than others, is there any country in which a woman is fully safe? As therapists seeing clients from different cultures, it appears that we can expect that women from most cultures carry a well-established Sexual Alarm System.

SUMMARY

How many sources of women's fear of their sexuality can there be? It goes on and on and includes many issues. This chapter has explored yet more of these issues including family history, motherhood, medical issues, lesbianism and bisexuality, and oppression of women in many cultures. Each of these issues can contribute to further entrenchment of the Sexual Alarm System in a woman's body and psyche. Part III presents ways of working with the Sexual Alarm System, beginning with chapter 8, which looks at how to go around the SAS.

III

Ways of Working with the Sexual Alarm System

Chapter Eight

Going Around the Sexual Alarm System

There is a direct and often successful approach to dealing with the SAS: finding behaviors that signal safety, in other words, behaviors that don't trigger the Alarm System. Imagine a house with an alarm, but there is a window that isn't wired. You could enter the house through that window and no alarm would sound. Women have these windows. This chapter presents ways of helping women to go around their SASs.

WHAT ARE THE WINDOWS?

These are some of the ways of going around the SAS often reported by women:

Looking me in the eye.
Talking with me.
Approaching me from the front.
Saying my name.
Touching me gently on first contact.
Sitting together holding hands.

What do these behaviors have in common? They are personal, slow, gentle, caring. They let the woman know that her partner is relating to her—not to a warm body for sex. These behaviors make connection. Most of all, they signal safety, which is essential for a woman to open up sexually. She cannot skip over this step and make herself be aroused by behaviors that scare her. It is unfair to her partner and to her that safety must come first, but that is the

59

way it works. I cannot emphasize this enough. Male partners and sometimes women partners complain, "Why can't she just 'do it'"? "Why does everything have to be just right?" "Why can't we just have good old sex once in awhile?" Simply because it doesn't work. The woman doesn't have control over her responses and she can be just as frustrated as her partner is with her reactions. Together partners need to learn to help the woman feel safe. This is the first of the Four Steps of Sexual Healing discussed in chapter 1.

Some windows into safety that open the way to sexuality are very individual. It is important for women to probe and experiment with finding alarm-free windows that can work for them. For example, one woman discovered that her window was going for a walk with her husband. The walk took her away from the laundry and the grocery list and therefore allowed her to be more in touch with her body and herself. Also, it gave her the opportunity to connect personally with her husband and to have safe physical contact with him.

Another woman would meditate prior to being sexual. Her woman partner would suggest being sexual and then she would go to meditate for twenty minutes. This time allowed her to sink into herself and her body, allowing the window to sexuality to open. A third woman would lie on her front and have her male partner put his hand on a certain spot in the middle of her back. She would then breathe into that spot allowing her body to relax and let go. Her partner would send his love into her body through his hand. After this, she was ready to open up sexually. In fact, prior to this experience, she was quite shut down and stuck, whereas after she could be easily aroused.

What is happening here? A number of factors are at play. In each instance the woman is finding a way into herself and her body. Many women live out their day giving out much of themselves to others and to what they do. They lose touch with themselves and their bodies. The experiences described above bring women back to themselves. This time allows them to collect their scattered pieces that are spread out during the day and also allows them to sense and feel their bodies. Too often women learn not to be in their bodies, certainly not sensually or sexually. It is sad that many women are critical of their bodies and experience them from the outside in rather than from the inside out. The emphasis on beauty, clothes, weight, makeup, and age teach women to see their bodies from the outside and constantly measure and judge themselves harshly. (As one woman said, "How can you have sex on top if your belly hangs down?") Women need to learn to experience their bodies from within and let go of external judgments, something very difficult to do.

Along with allowing a woman to find herself and her body, these experiences help her to make contact with her partner in a positive way. They help her tune into being with someone she loves rather than into danger. Her partner can then come in the window and the woman can feel safe.

If we think about everyday life as "A" and sex as "C," for many men life is full of references to "C." Ask a man how many times a day he thinks of something sexual. Ask a woman. There is not much in a woman's everyday life that entices her to think about sex. Women need a way to get from "A" to "C." I call this bridging or "B." These are ways of going around the SAS, of finding access to a woman's sexuality in a safe way. The above ways to go around the SAS are methods of bridging from "A" to "C." The pathway from "A" to "C" is often full of static, fear, and danger. Women need to find a bridge that is open and clear.

Below are experiences that are bridges from A to C and thus go around the SAS. They are presented as ideas you can give to your women clients and their partners.

1. Talk before being sexual to make connection. Talking allows you to connect personally with your partner and remember who you are with. Sit together on the couch or at the table. Share with each other personal reflections about the day.
2. Sit on the couch together and hold hands. Feel the contact and warmth of each other's hands. Take turns having one person explore the other's hands.
3. Sitting together or lying together on the bed, have your partner put his or her hand on your heart. Let the love pour through your partner's hand into your chest.
4. Cuddle together and stroke each other without the expectation of being sexual. This can take place on the couch or in bed. Women need to feel safe and not to feel they are just a body for their partner's sexual pleasure.
5. Sit across from each other in chairs. Without words take time to go into yourselves individually, closing your eyes. After you have quieted within yourself, gradually open your eyes and make eye contact. Resist the urge to talk to avoid the awkwardness and newness of just looking. Gaze into each other's eyes holding the gaze. Margo Anand (1989) calls this "soul gazing" (p.116). Notice how you feel and notice any tendency to disconnect. This exercise can allow a deep opening up between partners. It helps peel off the layers that separate them.
6. Lie together on the bed with clothes on at first. Begin some gentle touch that allows you to sink into your body. Guide the touching, sharing what feels safe and welcomed.
7. Have some small daily physical contact that allows you to feel connection without sexual pressure: a touch on the shoulder, a spontaneous hug, a light kiss.

8. Engage in some extended foreplay that involves eye contact, smiling, lightness, and lack of sexual pressure. Let this be very relaxing and pleasurable for both partners.
9. Engage in some physical play that takes down the SAS. Check in with yourself to find out which forms of play feel safe and don't trigger the SAS. Let yourself be silly, simple, gentle, even rambunctious together. Wendy Maltz (1991) introduces simple play exercises such as writing messages on each other's back with your hand for fun. Other forms of play are presented in the exercise sections that follow.

Numerous books discuss bridges to women's sexuality. Here are some examples from Bernie Zilbergeld's (1999) book *The New Male Sexuality*. *"Women attach great importance to words and talking"* (p. 112). *"For women, sex has meaning only in the context of a caring relationship"* (p.114). *"Women like men who are fully present and accounted for"* (p.114). *"Affectionate touching is very important to women"* (p.119).

These behaviors work because they go around the SAS, allowing a woman to find a path to her sexuality. Many woman experience a wide gulf between everyday life and sexuality. The SAS shuts a woman off from her sexuality. Men, on the other hand, have a great deal of permission to think about, look for, and hope for sexual stimulation. Think about those women in bikinis lounging on the sides of busses or the gorgeous lean women in the sexy underwear that arrive in catalogues at your house regularly. Sexuality is part of everyday life for many men. They would have to avoid it for it not to be. Men often think about it and make comments about it with other guys. There are certainly men who do not fit this description and for whom sexuality is a more private, personal, or even a distant, infrequent, or difficult experience.

Woman who relate with women partners also need bridging experiences. Brandy complained that her female partner Ally was like a train racing down the track. Brandy felt that Ally was moving so fast and so intensely toward the goal of orgasm that she wasn't relating to her. She needed Ally to slow down and allow her to feel safe by relating to her personally. She needed her SAS disarmed. Ally had a difficult time slowing down. Her mode was, as she put it, "quick and dirty." Intense and without much fuss was how she liked her sex. In fact, without knowing it, Ally was triggering Brandy's SAS because her way of relating sexually was non-personal and aggressive.

SEXUALITY AND SPIRITUALITY

Another way around the SAS for women is to connect their sexuality with their inner spirit. In the West, sexuality is often the antithesis of spirituality. I remember that when I first discovered the Tantric and Taoist concepts that sexuality is a most sacred way of expressing our connection to something greater than ourselves and that our bodies are a holy temple, I was astounded. I was raised in the Judeo-Christian tradition that connects sexuality with sin and severe restrictions for women. When I introduce Tantric concepts to women, they are immediately wondrous and intrigued. Why is this? Tantric is a broad holistic approach that includes mind, body, and spirit. It fits with Rosemary Basson's model that sexuality for women is part of a larger whole that includes intimacy. When women grasp the idea that their sexuality is a way of expressing sacred love, they feel safe, the first of the Four Steps of Sexual Healing. Many of the exercises in this book take women to a new freeing experience of their bodies. Through these experiences they can connect to an inner spirit that is quite divine and special. For more about connecting sexuality and spirituality, I refer you back to the discussion of Margo Anand's (1989) book *The Art of Sexual Ecstasy* in chapter 5.

CASE STUDY

Christina was turned off to sex with her husband. "Whenever he approaches me, I know where it is going. He wants sex, so I pull back inside." Like many women with male partners, she needed a sex-free transition time with her husband Jerome. She needed some "B" time in order that the SAS not be triggered. She needed some "B" time to come down into her body after hours of two young kids scrambling all over her. I gave them the assignment of cuddling in bed before going to sleep, with no sex resulting. Fortunately, Jerome knew that if he so much as mentioned anything about being sexual, the positive effects of the cuddling would be lost and Christina would go into Alarm mode. Like many women, once she felt assured of this time without sexual pressure, she relaxed and became open to physical contact and enjoyment. The cuddling was having the intended effect of going around the SAS. After a few weeks of this cuddling, Christina was ready to try sitting on the couch together and holding each other. Some time ago she had stopped this interaction because Jerome would reach for her crotch and she would freeze. With his assurance of not going for her crotch, she was ready and open to this next step. After a number of times of cuddling and holding each other on the couch, Christina began to feel more open and she experienced some desire. Caution! This is a tricky time because starved partners take this as a signal to run ahead and hope something sexual can happen. All can be lost if the partner pushes. Often the partner needs direction, reassurance, and time to vent his/her frustrations. Frequently this venting needs to be done in a therapy session by him- or herself. If the woman working on opening up hears about her partner's frustration, she will shut down. I worked with one couple in which every so often the husband let me know it was time for him to come in alone. Whoosh! Out came his frustration. Then he felt better and could continue with the work.

SUMMARY

It may be surprising how easy it can be to go around the SAS with the behaviors described above. They work because they signal safety and connection. They work because they let the woman know who she is with. And they work because they are not the behaviors associated with sexual violation. Because these behaviors are limited and don't address the underlying issues of the SAS, more approaches are needed for women.

And what about men? Where are men in this dilemma? Chapter 8 helps therapists talk with men about the SAS.

Chapter Nine

Addressing Men

This chapter is to help you, as a therapist, talk directly to heterosexual men. Getting men on board requires being able to speak to their concerns and feelings. You need to be able to speak their language. I have written this chapter as a conversation between therapists and men as an example of what has worked for me over many years of helping men understand the SAS and themselves. Each of us has our own style of addressing male heterosexual clients. I hope my conversation is helpful to you.

Talking with women partners is very different than talking with male partners because a woman partner has an SAS. If you are working with a lesbian couple, there may be some of this conversation that is adaptable to your client's woman partner, particularly in the "What Men Can Do" section. Clearly the conversation would need to be geared for the particular woman partner you are addressing.

TO MEN

You've tried. You've really tried to figure out what she likes sexually and to do the things she says will work for her. But they don't work. Or sometimes they work. But you don't know when. She says the best time is in the morning because she's not tired. But then in the morning she has too much on her mind and needs to get going. She says at night when everything is done. But everything is never done. She says to bring her flowers, to help her clean up the house. She even showed you that cute book *Porn for Women* (2007) . . . the one where the man vacuums the living room and gives her a massage. You do these things once in awhile, but you forget, plus the way you do them is often not quite right. It wasn't like this in the beginning. She was all over you. What happened?

It is not her fault. And it's not your fault. I want to help you learn about what is going on with her and why things go wrong between you by providing information on one of the underlying dynamics that interferes in sexual relationships with women, and by giving you suggestions about what you can do.

The Sexual Alarm System

Women have something called the Sexual Alarm System (SAS). Most men don't have anything like it, so it is hard to understand what makes your partner flinch away from you when you are trying to be sexy and enticing. Coming to understand this SAS will help you be able to work together with your partner toward a better sexual relationship.

The SAS is like a house alarm that surrounds a woman's body and goes off when she perceives that she is in danger. It is something that women have learned since they were children when people warned them about their sexual vulnerability. Little girls overhear comments like, "You better watch out for her when she grows up!" Watch out for what? Watch out for boys and men who would take advantage of them sexually. Many girls and young women have had actual experiences that have taught them firsthand of the dangers to them based on their sexuality. Probably your partner has had such experiences. Often women downplay or forget these experiences because they are so common. When they do this, they become unaware of the impact of what has happened to them. Imagine being followed, cornered, touched by men you don't know, and pushed into having sex. The bottom line is women's fear of sexual assault. Women who have not had any scary experiences know they are just around the corner. That is why they don't go out walking alone at 2 a.m., why they get nervous when a man enters an elevator and they are the only other person inside.

You have not grown up having to worry about a woman attacking you sexually. You don't think about a woman being a danger to you on an elevator, or on a street at night. When I point this out to men, some say, "I wish." For some men, it is a fantasy to have a strange woman push herself on to them sexually. Not for a woman. Men may be concerned about being mugged, but that is not about their sexuality. For the most part, men can go where they want, when they want, how they want without concern for their sexual safety. Because you don't have this experience of sexual fear, it is hard to know what a woman goes through and how much her sexual safety concerns permeate her life. It is hard to come up with a comparable experience that you may have had to let you know what a woman experiences.

Perhaps you were small as a boy and constantly worried about your size. Everywhere you went you were conscious of your body. Perhaps you had wet dreams and dreaded waking up to a gooey mess that might be discovered. Perhaps you are Arab and live in the US. If you are white, imagine how you would feel living in India or Africa. In fact, in a class on human sexuality, one man raised his hand and told the group that he knew about the SAS because he experiences it himself. People looked at him questioningly. How could he know? He said that he is a black man and that he experiences fear of sexual assault regularly. In fact, he is reminded by cars of white guys who lean out the window yelling sexual threats at him. It was a sobering moment for the class to understand that there is another group of people on this earth, a group of men, who have an SAS. There is another group of men who have an SAS: men who have experienced sexual abuse, particularly as children.

The SAS becomes part of a woman's instinctive reaction. It is lodged in a primal part of her brain that overrides her conscious thinking. It is a fight/flight response that is designed to protect her by signaling danger and overruling rational thought. It needs to react immediately. The SAS cannot discriminate who you are and why you are doing what you are doing. Thus, it is not under your partner's control. One man described walking into the kitchen toward his wife whose back was to him. She flinched without knowing it. A woman's reaction is just this quick and automatic. If she has had overt abuse, her reaction is going to be many times stronger.

Socially as a man, you have permission to be and are encouraged to be sexual. Bernie Zilbergeld (1999) writes, "Before they start having sex with partners or even themselves, boys know that sexual interest and prowess are crucial to being a man. The message permeates our culture" (p.11). Ads, movies, the internet, pornography, etc., entice you and tell you that you should want sex. The women in the pictures and videos all have perfect bodies and want sex . . . so they are portrayed. I have a male client whose wife who was infuriated that he had bought more pornography after promising not to. He tearfully explained that, "The women in the pictures want me." What he experienced with his wife was regular sexual rejection.

Male talk is often full of sexual references, boasting, and prowess. You may, in fact, suffer from this pressure to measure up to the "player" image. Or you may have been raised with negative religious and/or family views of sexuality that keep you sexually inhibited or conflicted. So, the picture for men is certainly not all affirmative. For example, you may feel vulnerable to your woman partner because you have been raised to feel accepted or rejected by her response to you sexually.

Whereas you are, however, expected and pushed to be sexual, women are challenged to be sexy, but discouraged from being sexual. This can be very confusing for you. Women want sexual attention, but they do not necessarily want to be sexual. When you are young and in your twenties, sex can be very exciting and women seem thoroughly on board. There are women ready for "hooking up," ready to give oral sex, ready to have intercourse when you first start dating. It is later when intimacy develops and commitment happens that women change. How many men complain about how their wife's attitude toward sexuality changed the day they got married. If not then, when she had her first child. When you are young, her excitement and wish to be desired override her SAS. She may be reacting more to your attention than to the sex. Or she may be really enjoying the sex because it is new and outside of the strictures of what she is supposed to be. The fear and inhibitions catch up to her when she relaxes into a more real self. How sad for both of you.

Growing up, you are likely to have been well-trained by your male peers to be very careful about touch. You shake hands with men. You high-five each other. You bump each other and clap each other on the back. As teens, you wrestled and pushed each other. McCarthy and Metz (2008) explain, "Locker-room teasing, joking about another man, and exaggerating sexual escapades are accepted as normal male interaction" (p. 8). Zilbergeld (1999) writes:

> Since strength and self reliance are the primary goals we have for our males, they are trained to mistrust and dislike the more vulnerable and expressive side of themselves. Boys are rewarded for "toughing it out," "hanging tough," not crying, not being weak . . . Part of being tough is not getting or needing the loving touching that all babies get. Parents stop touching their boys early on. (pp. 7–8)

Perhaps you were fortunate enough to have grown up in a family or a subculture in which men could show affection. They could hug and put a hand on each other's shoulder. This is not the experience of many men in this culture. Women, on the other hand, play with each other's hair, hug regularly, hold hands, lean on each other. They are warm and soft. Now she wants this from you? In the beginning of relating to her, this kind of touch may come more naturally because you are in love and because it is a way to win her. Now you may have retreated back to your old ways . . . just as she has. You think patting her on the butt, surprising her from behind with your arms around her shoulders, tweaking her nipples will excite her as it does you. When she objects, you tell her you are just playing, that she is making too big a deal out of it. Doesn't she get it? She is way overly sensitive. This is the SAS at work. Unbeknownst to you, you are triggering her that she is in danger.

But you're not like those guys out there! You don't follow women, expose yourself, or act sexually threatening. You would never do those things to a woman! Why do you have to suffer for what other men do? There is no question that your partner's reaction is unfair to you. Both of you realize this is part of how you can get on the same page together. You are not a dangerous man and yet she reacts to you as if you are. You didn't cause this reaction and she is not choosing it. She is well trained to protect herself and she had better be for her own safety. Would you want her out alone at 2 o'clock in the morning?

Knowing about these issues and the SAS can bring and your partner great relief. You have probably tried to say things like, "Don't you know it's me" when she flinches as you approach her, or "Why can't you just relax and enjoy it" when you pat her on the bum. When you get frustrated, you may say, "I don't understand your problem. You are so uptight. What is the matter with you?" This book can help you work together by understanding why she reacts the way she does, by knowing that neither of you causes the problem, and by discovering that you can work together to change what is happening.

TO THERAPISTS

When I first started talking to men in this way, I feared their reaction would be anger or alienation. In fact, they are *relieved* when I speak to them about their experiences, women's experiences, and what they go through relating to women sexually. They need to feel understood and they need to see the bigger picture in order to feel less rejected, less angry, and more supportive of their woman partner. My conversations with them do help them realize that what happens is not their fault and not the woman's fault. Then together they can address the SAS as a team. Use whatever ideas from here that can help you work with your male heterosexual clients. Adjust the conversation to fit your style and your particular male client.

CASE STUDY

Sex had pretty much dropped out of Reba and Aaron's life. Aaron was mystified wondering what happened. In their first years, they couldn't get enough of each other sexually. Reba wanted him as much as he wanted her. Gradually her responsiveness declined and she seemed to avoid contact with Aaron. He still tried to get her interested because sometimes it worked. He never knew what would turn her on. Not that he hadn't tried to figure it out. He even bought her some Victoria's Secret lingerie for her birthday. She told him he bought it for his pleasure and not for her. She complained that she was just a body for him to have sex with. But, that wasn't true. He wanted *her*. She acted like he was a letch when he touched her breasts. He had been so careful not to be like her last boyfriend who pushed her constantly to be sexual and berated her for looking so pretty and delivering so little. So, Aaron spent time talking with Reba before he suggested sex. He complimented her on her body. Couldn't she see how much he was trying to make sex work together? Reba and Aaron needed to learn about the SAS. He was clearly doing things that triggered her without knowing it. When Aaron and Reba came to understand that her reaction wasn't personal, they began to give a sigh of relief and join together to take steps to help Reba with her SAS. They became allies. Together they learned what Reba's SAS triggers were and how to adapt to them.

WHAT MEN CAN DO

Many men will say, "Just tell me what to do. I've tried everything and nothing works." So here are some concrete steps that you as a therapist can give to men. I present them as a conversation with your male heterosexual clients.

1. Talk to your woman partner about the SAS. Show interest. Invite her to tell you about her experiences and the experiences of other women who have affected her. Zilbergeld (1999) advises men, "*Women appreciate men who listen to them and take them seriously*" (p. 115). Encourage her to tell her stories. She may be reluctant because she hasn't fully realized herself the significance of her experiences or because she thinks you will dismiss her concerns. Assure her that you want to understand. Encourage her to tell you what it is like for her when she hears constant news stories of girls' abductions, boyfriends attacking and raping girlfriends, famous men cheating on their women. Watch out for getting defensive. Remember these men are not you.

2. Don't try to fix her concerns. Don't dismiss them as due to a few jerks and crazy men. Imagine what she goes through inside. Try to empathize by saying things like, "That must have been scary." McCarthy and Metz (2008) write, "To empathize with your partner, imagine for a moment that you are her. Imagine that you think and feel as she does, that you experience her reality" (p. 28). If you are not so good at empathy, just listen. Be sure in no way to blame her by saying such things as, "You shouldn't have been out there at night" or, "Don't get into the elevator if the guy looks creepy."

3. Help her ferret out the triggers to her SAS. Ask her what they are. Be prepared to be surprised by triggers that you would not have guessed. Think about any triggers that you can see. Know that some of them are probably things you do and remember that her reaction is not your fault. Your behavior is triggering deeper fears about her sexual safety. You might read about triggers in chapter 2 so that you can know what

are common triggers for women. Ask other women too, such as your sisters and your women friends. In fact, it could be helpful to talk to them first to practice and so that you can be more objective. You might have to explain the SAS to them.

4. Learn ways to go around the SAS. These include the following (see chapter 8):

- If she is uncomfortable being approached from behind, make sure you approach her from the front.
- If she doesn't like it when the first thing you do is grab her breasts, touch her on her shoulders when you first make contact.
- Make a personal connection with her before attempting to be sexual. This allows her to feel safe and avoids triggering the SAS. Talk with her, cuddle with her, massage her feet, or touch her face. Let her know that it is you.
- Say her name when you first approach her and interact with her. This lets her know it is you.
- Look her in the eye when you come to her. Show her warmth with your face. Again, this lets her know it is you and that you care about her.

5. If she is working with the exercises in this book, honor her work by encouraging her, but not overly so or she'll take this as pressure. Don't ask her too often how she is doing with the exercises or what she is doing. She needs to have these experiences as her own and not feel you are taking them over. Read about what she is doing in this book.

6. For your own sanity in getting through this, read the chapter about adding arousal so that you can see that there is hope. Also, this will help you be prepared when she gets to this point.

7. Read about women's sexual issues, not only here but also in other books such as *Reclaiming Desire* by Goldstein and Brandon (2004). There are also very helpful chapters on relating to women in Zilbergeld's (1999) *The New Male Sexuality*. It is important that you be informed if you are to be understanding. McCarthy and Metz (2008) emphasize the importance of being an intimate team with your partner.

There are also important things that you as a therapist can suggest for men to do for themselves. This journey can be hard on men—frustrating, discouraging, and lonely. They need direction and support. Here are some strategies to suggest to men.

1. Find an outlet for your frustration. Telling your woman partner is not it. She feels guilty and helpless enough. You need someone you can vent to and get support from for your concerns. It may be foreign for you to talk about your feelings. So, who can you talk with? A good friend, a therapist, another man who shares your experience. I have several male clients I see in couples therapy who once every several months need to come in to let out their frustration and get some hope for where this is all going. They need to know that someone gets where they are in this journey since the focus is so much on the woman's healing.

2. Even though your partner is not a good source of support, she does need to know that her issues affect you and that you are trying to handle your feelings. If she knows that you understand and support her healing, she will be more likely to show you some understanding. Her defensiveness usually is the result of her own guilt, sexual pressure she feels, and any blaming that comes from you. Tell her about how hard this is from a caring place and from your pain, not your anger. Sharing pain and loneliness is not easy for men. They are more vulnerable emotions. She is likely to be able to hear them better than your anger.

3. What do you do with your sexual needs? Find a constructive way to deal with them until your partner is ready to be sexual with you. She may be able to be sexual at times or not at all while she is learning to experience her body and her sexual feelings safely. Many men masturbate during this time to release their sexual tensions. Yes, it is not very satisfying. You want to be sexual with your wife/partner. It at least allows you to recognize and take care of your own needs.

4. Recognize your vulnerability to other nonconstructive outlets for your sexuality. Stay conscious. This is one of your greatest vulnerabilities: to become unconscious and oblivious, to act automatically without thinking about the consequences. Be careful of falling into an affair. You may even feel entitled to being sexual with another woman with what you "have to put up with." An affair is going to make things very messy and bring in whole other issues such as trust from which you may well not recover as a couple. And pornography? Also be watchful of how much you use, particularly internet pornography, which is so available and compelling. It can get all too easy to spend hours on the net. Porn addiction has become a major issue in these times. Some porn use may be helpful depending in part on how your partner feels about it. Extensive secretiveness is not helpful.

5. Learn more about your own sexuality as a man: what drives you, what you want, how you have been conditioned, and what experiences you have had that affect your sense of yourself as a man. I highly recom-

mend the above mentioned book *The New Male Sexuality* by Bernie Zilbergeld (1999). He speaks directly to men about their experiences around sexuality, exposing the myths of male sexuality and looking at sexual issues for men. I suggest you read those sections that may apply to you and skip those that don't. Most men to whom I recommend this book can't put it down.

SUMMARY

Men too suffer because of the SAS. They don't understand it and they don't know what to do with it because most of them don't experience it. This chapter gives you, as a therapist, a direct conversation to have with men to help them to gain understanding of the SAS: how it works, their own reaction to it, and what to do to address it. There are important steps that they can take to help their woman partner, to be a team together, and to handle their own needs and feelings. Neither partner caused the SAS. In their relationships men and women can work together to develop ways of interacting that minimize and go around the SAS, thus building the trust and safety that women need to be open to sexual experience. Chapters 11 and 12 develop a wide array of exercises for therapists to help women be in their bodies. These chapters are introduced in the next chapter, which gives an overview of the exercises.

Chapter Ten

The Exercises

An Overview

How does a woman learn to be more comfortable in her body in order to welcome in sexual arousal and diminish the unwanted effects of the SAS? The SAS shuts women down sexually. To counter this, this chapter introduces two categories of exercises that I have developed for therapists to use to help women open up their bodies and prepare them for sexual feelings. Many of these exercises are unique in the way that they help women be in their bodies. These exercises are designed to help women with two of the important Four Steps of Sexual Healing described in chapter 1: establishing safety and owning one's own female sexuality.

BACKGROUND

As a young therapist and a student of dance, yoga, martial arts, and other forms of movement, it occurred to me that there are many types of movements and other experiences that comprise the sexual experience. Being aroused is only one part of being sexual. So, I thought, what if women could learn these movements and sensations without the arousal? Then when they add the arousal, they would be much more likely to be receptive to the sexual feelings. As a result, I developed and ran for many years a one-and-a-half-day workshop called Body Work for Sexual Health and Healing. A central part of this workshop was taking women through various physical aspects of the sexual experience without the sexual arousal. Learning to open the body in various ways without arousal increases the possibility that the SAS is not triggered. A woman can learn many of the aspects of being sexual that are essential to the experience without the scary and difficult parts. Later when arousal is added, the woman can already feel comfortable and safe. The safe parts of the experience can welcome in the arousal.

This level of work involves retraining the body and creating new body learning. It is vital for rediscovering the basic primal elements of the sexual experience without the arousal. The SAS is not likely to be triggered. When a woman can come to know her body in such a primal and positive way, she is empowered and she is creating new instinctual responses.

As previously described, there are many books and approaches to help women get in touch with their sexuality. This approach is different in its concept and behavioral treatment. Some approaches focus specifically on ways to directly access sexuality. These approaches include the use of masturbation, visual sexual images, and sexual fantasies. For many women these approaches are very helpful, but for some women they may be too direct and charged. These women need to overcome emotional and physical obstacles first. The approach developed in this book is unique in 1) recognizing and naming the Sexual Alarm System and 2) developing and organizing exercises that address the SAS. Here I am focusing on a primal negative response to sexuality for women. There are other levels of women's negative responses to sexuality such as the good girl syndrome, the incompatibility of motherhood and sexuality, and the belief that sex is evil. These levels touch on values, beliefs, expectations, priorities. They are cognitive, social, religious, etc. The SAS is connected to these experiences and an integral part of them. What makes the SAS distinct is its interweaving with our instincts and therefore our automatic responses.

Something vital is left out if a woman's sexual healing does not address this primal instinctual level. Doing sexual healing work without this primal work would be like helping someone deal with the fear of fire without addressing the basic human instinct to protect ourselves from something that can cause us harm. We can learn to build fires, extinguish fires, and make fireplaces. To be completely confident to deal with fire, we need to face its danger and our instinct to pull away from it and run. Sex is like fire. It is exciting, enlivening, destructive, scary. It is intriguing, unpredictable, elemental, wild, explosive, quiet, intoxicating. Fire gives light and warmth. It keeps us from freezing and dying. Sex too is a life force that brings energy and life. It too can get out of control and claim us as its victim.

THE PROGRAM OF EXERCISES

Because of the presence of the SAS, the exercises I have developed are for all women. First I address the many movements that make up the sexual experience without the arousal. Below in Table 10.1 is a list of specific body actions that I have developed into exercises for women. I call these the Ingredients.

There is a second part to the work that helps a woman become more physically open and deal with the SAS. In addition to the Ingredients, there needs to be an order of progression of body experiences that allows a woman to open up and take in the Ingredients. This progression needs to proceed through successive steps that gradually help her to experience her body more fully. I call these the Progressive Exercises.

For a woman to open in the most receptive way, she needs to go though the following four steps: Awakening, Awareness, Allowing, and Surrender. Awakening brings the body to life. When a woman's body has been shut down by the SAS, she needs movement that brings her to her body's sensations. These movements need to gently prod the body to wake up and notice. Sometimes the prodding needs to be more of a push to get the woman's attention.

Once she is awakened, she needs to be aware of what she is experiencing. Exercises that sustain her attention and sensation foster Awareness. A woman needs to be able to focus and deepen her experience. Exercises that are continuous and somewhat repetitive help the most.

Once a woman is aware, she needs to let her experience develop and grow. I call this Allowing because she needs to permit her sensations to move and expand. Exercises that have a continuous and shifting flow work well for

Table 10.1. The Ingredients

Breathing	Sliding and Gliding
Sounds	Rolling
Receiving Touch	Thrusting
Making Faces	Feeling out of Control
Licking	Vibrating/Jiggling
Tingling/Electric Sensations	Shaking
Spreading	Total Body Shaking
Expanding	Undulating/Writhing
Rocking	Thrashing

Allowing. These exercises tend to involve more movement on the part of the woman in order to facilitate the developing flow. This can be an exciting time for a woman as she feels something new expanding in her body.

Then comes Surrender, which involves a full letting go. It is the time when the movement takes over and a woman's body guides her experience. The mind is finally quiet as she immerses herself into her sensations. These movements are usually more vigorous so that the resulting responses can fill the body. Surrendering is different than just feeling out of control. It involves a sense of release, abandon, and transcendence. Margo Anand (1989) writes of the importance of surrender in learning to fully experience your sexual energy. She points out the confusion people have between submission and surrender. Submission, "implies giving up responsibility for one's behavior" (p. 46) whereas "the true meaning of *surrender* is to melt into that which is higher than yourself" (p. 46).

Thus, there are two parts to the exercises presented here. First are the exercises for the dimensions of being sexual without the arousal. These are the "Ingredients." Examples include Rocking, Sliding, and Writhing. Secondly, a program of exercises is presented that focuses on a gradual development moving from Awakening to Awareness to Allowing to Surrender. I call this the Progressive Exercises. Included in each of the four levels of the Progressive Exercises are appropriate exercises drawn from the Ingredients as well as other helpful exercises. As an example, Thrashing, one of the Ingredients, is a good exercise for the Surrender level of the Progressive Exercises. Below is an outline to summarize the two programs of exercises.

Chapter 11: The Ingredients: movements and exercises for the dimensions of being sexual without arousal.

Chapter 12: The Progressive Exercises

1. Awakening
2. Awareness
3. Allowing
4. Surrender

There is clearly overlap between the subcategories of the Ingredients and the Progressive Exercises. However, I have separated them because they are not exactly the same. The Ingredients spell out very specific movements and exercises that dissect the dimensions of the sexual experience. The Progressive Exercises are comprised of a succession of movements and body experiences that gradually open up a woman's body.

None of these exercises are hard to do. They are not complicated or physically demanding. In that sense "exercises" may be a misnomer. Experiences is a more apt term. The challenge of the exercises is in their newness, their awkwardness, and their ability to open up unknown experiences. Primarily they can be fun, freeing, and releasing.

Although the exercises are about body movements, women are led to experience both their physical and their emotional reactions. Throughout the exercises I encourage women to relax, to go inward, and to feel. I discuss how the exercises help women be in touch with a sense of safety and with their inner spirit. If women experience the exercises only on a physical level, they will not have much effect. The integration of body, mind, and spirit is crucial. This is what female sexuality is all about.

HOW TO USE THE EXERCISES

As a therapist, you can take several paths in helping women use these exercises: 1) you can guide women through the Ingredients exercise by exercise; 2) you can guide women through the Progressive Exercises step by step to experience each level of opening the body in order; or 3) from both lists you can pick and choose those exercises that are most appropriate for each client. This third option is the one followed in this book. You can help a woman design and/or find her own path that works for her body. The main direction is to help her to open her body and herself for new and familiar sensations that build her ability to deal with the SAS and lead the way to opening sexually.

I like to think of this work as a detective hunt. We want to help a woman find a window into her sensations and responsiveness. We want to help her find a way around and through the SAS. We have clues from other women and from knowledge of the SAS. But we don't know just what is going to work for a particular woman, that is, which exercises will help deal with her SAS.

The exercises are done at home in a comfortable setting conducive to opening up and letting go. You can help your woman client decide whether to be clothed, partly clothed, or unclothed. When she first starts it is better to be clothed or partly clothed in order to feel safe and not trigger the SAS.

Take stock of any physical limitations a woman may have that may influence which exercises she can comfortably do. Certainly she should not do anything that is going to strain her. Her health is primary.

Women often need a woman guide on this journey because it is very hard to keep going alone. The detective hunt may be daunting, depressing, and get stuck easily. As the therapist, you can guide women, help them recognize clues, help keep confidence in the process, and be a cheerleader. You can 1) tell by a woman's response that she is on the right path even when she has doubts; 2) tell stories of other women, helping your client feel connected to other women; 3) normalize and educate; and 4) be a model with your energy, your own journey, and your belief in the process. You have been there and can lead the way along the path by example, keeping appropriate boundaries. Because the SAS is necessary and ever active, the journey doesn't end. Dealing with the SAS is not something you learn and then you are done. Since the SAS continues to function, we need to keep active in countering it, working through it, and going around it. A guide on the paths directs, listens, and shares. She also learns since we all need to continue to grow. Each woman's journey reinforces the paths of the guides. Against all the forces that necessitate the existence of the SAS, we have much to learn, to share, and to spread to each other. This book is a guide that you as a therapist can use to help your women clients. Women can also use the book by themselves.

Male therapists can work with women using these exercises if they are experienced and comfortable working with women and women's sexual issues and if the woman client trusts the male therapist. In doing this work male therapists need to be especially clear about the boundaries of the work, letting the woman client know directly that her exercises are to be done only at home and not in the office. Therapists who are not sex therapists can use these exercises if they are experienced in working with women's sexual issues and are comfortable and knowledgeable about processing women's responses to this type of body work.

As a clinician who will suggest these exercises to women clients, it is vital that you experience the exercises yourself before you use them with clients. Knowing your own reactions and feelings through these experiences can be an important guide for you in working with women. Your comfort with the exercises is important to convey to your clients. They will pick up on your ability to relate to the exercises and their experiences with them. Have fun and open yourself for a wonderful journey to enhance your own life!

WHAT TO DO ABOUT SEX WHILE DOING THE EXERCISES

What does a woman do about sex while she is working on the exercises in this book? If she has a partner, she can choose whether to be sexual with him or her or not. If she has enough of a satisfying sex life with her partner, there may be no need to alter what she is doing while she is trying out this new work. It is important, however, to keep these exercises separate from being sexual. I would also suggest that a woman not bring this work into her couple sexual life until she has felt some change and has developed confidence in her new experiences. Some women may want or need to stop being sexual with their partner while working on the exercises in this book. A sexual break may be helpful to enable women to really focus on this work and not have their SAS being triggered while working to diminish and control it. Taking a break will clearly affect the relationship and needs to be discussed with a woman's partner. She or he will likely have feelings about such a change and needs to understand what the woman is doing and how it can help.

SUMMARY

This chapter introduces the next two chapters, which give the primary ways of countering the SAS. The SAS involves women shutting down and withdrawing. These exercises help women come alive and be in their bodies. What a turnaround!

Chapter Eleven

Experiencing All the Dimensions of Sexuality without the Arousal

The Ingredients

Breathing, Rocking, Thrashing. Where does a woman begin and how does she become comfortable with these experiences? This chapter presents the Ingredients of the sexual experience without the arousal. It may surprise you how many movements there are that are part of being sexual. Each exercise is presented with the goal, preparation, and directions to make the exercises accessible and clear. They are written as directions to your client from you, the therapist. These exercises are more windows into a woman's sexuality. They help build safety and they help women build a much stronger sense of their own female sexuality, two of the four Steps of Sexual Healing described in chapter 1. First explain to your woman client the concept of experiencing the dimensions of sexuality without the arousal. Then choose those exercises that you think best fit where your woman client is in her journey. Present her with a number of options and explore her reactions to those options. Together find exercises that feel comfortable to her at the beginning. As she gains experience with some exercises, suggest other exercises that are a slight stretch for her so she can expand her experience. Be sure to check with her that the exercises she chooses are ones she can physically do without discomfort. Once your client has chosen a couple of exercises to try, go through the goal, the preparation, and the directions as given below. Feel free to adjust the exercises to fit your client's needs.

THE INGREDIENTS

Breathing

Breathing is the very life of movement. It is the impulse, the taking in, the letting go, the enlivening. It is the fundamental basis of awakening and sustaining energy and responsiveness. Without it there is no energy or life. So how is it that we disregard it, take it for granted, even stifle it? Even when we are sexual, we choke off our breathing by ignoring it, breathing minimally, or even holding our breath when we could expand our experience by fully participating in our breathing. It is so simple. We just need to breathe more fully and rhythmically and feel the energy moving through our bodies. By doing this, we experience our bodies and our sexual responses more fully. We are not used to this. In sex we strive for a limited genital experience, not a full-bodied experience. For many women this limited genital experience does not work. The SAS blocks women's sensations and does it well. Breathing is a primary tool that women can use to deal with the SAS because it makes it harder for the SAS to do its job. In other words, when women breathe fully and feel their energy moving openly, the SAS is not as effective. The SAS depends on body constriction and on fear. Breathing does two essential things that seem to be opposite. It at once relaxes us and energizes us. Tantric and Taoist approaches to sexuality focus strongly on breathing techniques in order to open us up to our full sexual experience. Margo Anand (1989) writes:

> Many forms of spiritual practice and methods of self-development place great emphasis on breathing . . . in a slow and conscious way . . . deep breathing is what connects us to our sexual centers. The deeper we breathe, the more we come into contact with our sexual energy. (p. 51)

> When your respiration becomes more active, your energy level rises, and the nerve endings beneath your skin become more sensitive, resulting in a sense of tingling and vibrancy. (p. 130)

Tantra teaches us the importance of breathing to feel fully sexual. Think about how often when we go to hug someone, we hold our breath. This stops us from feeling the other's body and from responding. There are many wonderful breathing exercises from a number of Eastern techniques that we can use to enhance our sexual experience. Several of these are included below. Here are five different breathing exercises you can suggest to your woman client.

1. Simple Breathing

Goal: To feel and expand your breathing more fully.

Preparation: Sit upright in a comfortable chair or lie on a mat or carpet on the floor in a relaxing environment.

Directions: Begin with the most simple breathing exercise, conscious inhaling and exhaling. Lying down on a bed, draw the air in through your nose expanding your belly as you do. This can be challenging for women because we are supposed to keep our bellies flat. Feel the air entering your diaphragm, your chest, and your pelvis. Then exhale and feel the air flowing out of your pelvis, diaphragm, and chest. As your body releases, feel a letting go. Put your hand on your chest and belly to sense the movement of these areas as you inhale and exhale. Feel yourself coming alive.

2. Genital Breathing

Goal: To connect your breathing to your genitals.

Preparation: Sit upright in a comfortable chair or lie on a mat or carpet on the floor in a relaxing environment.

Directions: Now add your genitals to the above breathing (Who thinks about their genitals when breathing?). Imagine your vagina and vulva to be like a mouth. As you inhale, imagine drawing air into your vagina and letting it expand and relax. As you exhale, imagine that you are pushing the air out through your vagina. Be aware of the sensations in your genitals and pelvis as you do this. The first few times you do this, it may feel awkward. You may feel nothing. Keep doing the exercise as this takes time to experience.

The idea of genital breathing seemed ridiculous to Lily. She hardly experienced her genitals as there. So, the first step was to awaken her awareness that she had genitals by doing contracting and releasing of her pelvic floor muscles, otherwise known as Kegel exercises. This helped her to feel sensations in a lost part of her body. No one had ever spoken of her genitals, her vagina, or her pelvic floor. After a few weeks of doing Kegels regularly, she was ready to try the genital breathing. Lying on her bed she focused on inhaling and opening her vagina as she relaxed, then exhaling as she contracted her vagina. It took her some practice to get the flow of it. Gradually she was able to feel an awakening in her pelvic floor. With great excitement she came in to a session one day and proclaimed that she now knew she had genitals. They really existed!

3. Pelvic Rock Breathing

This is a potentially powerful breathing and rocking exercise. It takes some coordination and practice before it flows smoothly.

Goal: To open up your pelvis to increased sensation and to connect pelvic movements to your breathing.

Preparation: Lie on a carpet or mat on the floor on your back, with your knees up and your feet on the floor in a comfortable environment.

Directions:

Step 1: Do the above Genital Breathing.

Step 2: Now focus just on moving your pelvis in the following way: Arch your back up at the waist rocking your genitals toward the floor. Then reverse the movement flattening your back down and very slightly raising your lower buttocks off the floor.

Step 3: Now combine steps 1 and 2 so that as you arch your back up and rock your genitals toward the floor, you relax and open your vagina imagining that you inhale through it. Imagine that you are making a space for the air to enter your pelvis. Then exhale as you flatten your back and pull your lower buttocks up very slightly, imagining that you can exhale through your vagina.

Think: arch, open, and inhale, then flatten, contract and exhale. Feel the sensations in your genitals as you breathe and rock!

Heiman and LoPiccolo (1988) describe a similar exercise that they call "the rocking pelvis" (p. 70). Loulan (1984) gives an example of opening and closing the genitals as a way of letting go of tension (p. 225). Kegel exercises, the contracting and releasing of the pelvic floor often taught for childbirth (Berman & Berman, 2005), are an important aspect of this exercise.

In my workshop, Body Work for Sexual Health and Healing, the pelvic breathing was a staple exercise. Some women struggled to coordinate the different steps. Often the women needed to focus so much on how to do the exercise that they did not initially feel the opening of their pelvic area. Some could feel it right away. For most it took practice before their bodies began to move into a rhythmic flow. Two weeks later the women would return for a half-day follow-up session having practiced the exercises on their own. This exercise particularly needs practice. It can take a woman into a new and different feeling in her pelvis and can open up sexual sensations in a freeing and unthreatening way. One woman came to me after the workshop to continue the breathing work. She loved the pelvic breathing exercise because it helped her to stop, focus, move, and breathe. She loved being surprised at how much sensation she could generate in her previously dead-feeling pelvis. At home she would rock her pelvis as she let out marvelous sounds as she exhaled.

4. Panting

Goal: To build your level of comfort with an increased and intense energy flow through your body and with the sensations that accompany this flow.

Preparation: Sit in an upright comfortable chair or walk around your house or run up and down stairs.

Directions: Panting involves short rapid in and out breaths through your nose. It often occurs during the sexual buildup of arousal. Practice panting by sitting in a chair and taking the rapid in and out breaths. You might feel some lightheadedness. You can also try panting while walking in your house. Notice how you feel as you pant. It may be more comfortable to try panting as a result of exercise. For example, you can run up and down the stairs to induce panting. Feel the adrenaline and awakening that you generate doing this. Panting prepares you for the next powerful exercise.

5. Breath of Fire

Goal: To experience a powerful yoga breathing technique that fully energizes your body.

Preparation: Sit in a comfortable position, for example, on the floor with legs crossed (if you can) or in an upright armless chair in a relaxing environment.

Directions: With a big inhale, raise your arms over your head in a "V" shape. Stick your tongue out and pant like a dog. This teaches the breath. Now close your mouth and inhale and exhale through your nose slowly with strong breaths using your belly. Expand your belly as you inhale and contract it as you exhale. Begin to slowly increase the speed of your breaths. As your speed picks up feel the energy blasts into your chest. Your breaths are becoming more rapid and short. Keep increasing the speed until you are breathing rapidly. Stay at a high speed for a minute or so. When you are ready to stop, take one last long inhale and hold your breath with your arms up. Pause in this position and then exhale and lower your arms. Take a few minutes to sit and feel the incredible energy and awakening that you have generated. Let the energy course throughout your body. You may feel tingling, light-headedness, and an electric feeling. To see a variation of the Breath of Fire go to www.youtube.com/watch?v=CB7v3tHow_o.

Sounds

There is a wonderful scene that recurs in an Italian movie. In the courtyard of an apartment building where many activities take place, there periodically comes the sound of a woman having an orgasm. What is particularly remarkable about these occurrences is that the people in the courtyard either enjoy the sound or are not fazed by it. In our culture we are uncomfortable with sexual noises. Particularly women are taught not to make noise during sex . . . it might mean they are enjoying the sex. Yet, allowing sounds to come out can greatly enhance sexual experience. In fact, if sounds don't emerge, we probably aren't breathing, or at least breathing fully. How does one not make a sound when a wonderful cathartic experience is happening?

Learning to make sounds separately from sex will help allow women to release sounds that they can later add to the sexual experience. Margo Anand (1989) writes, "let yourself sigh, shout and cry as the spirit moves you. Don't censor your vocal expression; . . . And when it comes to making love, you will experience a world of difference between silent sex—restraining the sounds—and expressing your feelings in sound . . ." (p. 131). Following are some sound exercises to suggest to your women clients.

Goals for the following exercises: To experience the sensations and joy of making and releasing sounds. To experiment with different sounds.
Preparations: Sit upright in a comfortable chair in a quiet, relaxing environment.
Directions:

1. Begin with the above Simple Breathing exercise. Add sound to it when you exhale, just a simple "Ahhh." Feel the vibration of the sound in your chest. Feel how it amplifies your breathing, allowing it to be more full and expansive.
2. Try rapid breathing in and out accompanied by sounds. Let the sounds be voiced breaths using your vocal cords. Again experience how the sounds intensify your breathing.
3. Let some sighs come out as you exhale. Feel your body let go with each sigh. Let your shoulders come down as you relax with each breath.
4. Try making different fun sounds like clucking, whistling, blowing, chirping, growling, meowing, barking, lip smacking, cawing, howling, cheering. With each sound feel the quality of it as it resonates in your body. See which sounds are the most satisfying and enjoyable. Now make sounds of satisfaction such as "mmmm" and moans such as "ohhh."
5. Combine making sounds with other exercises in this chapter such as Shaking, Rocking, and Thrusting.

Receiving Touch

Being able to sense touch is crucial to the sexual experience both alone and with a partner. It is one of the building blocks of intimacy and sexuality.

Goal: To experiment with different types of self touch to experience what you like and how you respond.

Preparation: Sit upright in a comfortable chair in a relaxing environment. Have your arms uncovered.

Directions:

Self-Caressing: First hold your hands together. Feel the warmth of your skin on each hand. Feel the softness and the intimacy of this holding. Breathe in and sink into the sensations. Now using one hand, place your palm over the back of your other hand. Stay there a moment. Then move your top hand slowly up your arm gently caressing your arm. Self-Caressing involves a slow tender sliding movement up and down the skin. Continue this caressing on the under part of your forearm and up the under side of your upper arm. Take in this caring touch as you feel your skin.

Kneading: Now with one hand begin to gently knead your other hand. Use your thumb to press into your muscles, plying them and massaging them. Continue up your arm letting your muscles receive this loosening touch and release. Go all over your arm with this motion.

Scratching: With your fingertips and nails, gently and lightly scratch your arm, stimulating the skin and bringing it alive. Feel the slight sharpness of this touch awakening your skin. Go all over your arm taking your time.

Finger touch: Slide your fingers over your arm barely touching it with the pads of your fingers. Feel the lightness and bare presence of this touch all over your arm.

Now do the same four touches with the other hand on the other arm.
At the end sit and take in which type of touch you liked the best and why. Then go back to this type of touch and repeat it. When done, sit and absorb the sensations on your arm.

All over body: Now that you have tried different types of touch, let yourself experiment with touching different parts of your body with the four different touches. For example, you may want to caress your chest area and/or knead your calf muscles. Let these be pleasant pleasuring experiences. Be aware of any feelings that may get in your way of relaxing into your touch.

Making Faces

The look of excitement, surprise, pushing, building up tension, focusing, loving, connecting, releasing, exploding! Our faces are an integral part of the sexual experience. Who would think of making sexual faces, yet we do it spontaneously during sex. What is a sexual face? It is many different expressions. It could be fun for a woman to find out.

> *Goal:* To experiment with making facial expressions that occur while being sexual and to have some fun.
>
> *Preparation:* Sit in a comfortable chair in a private relaxed environment. Have a mirror available nearby.
>
> *Directions:* Imagine a positive sexual experience that you have had. Imagine the steps of the experience letting yourself make the facial expressions you may have made. You may feel quite silly doing this. Then play with different facial expressions that you could make during sex including those listed above.

Let other parts of your body accompany your facial expressions. For example, when you scrunch your face up as if you are pushing, feel the pushing in your shoulders and back too. Play with these movements, letting yourself be silly. The point of this exercise is NOT to make you more self-conscious, but to widen your expressiveness. If you are in a mode of having fun, you might look at yourself in the mirror while making expressions, but only if this helps you enjoy the exercise.

Licking

Well, what do we do with licking? It seems so sensual. Think of the pleasures of licking. Ice cream, the sauce off the plate, the juice of the peach on our fingers. How often do we lick for reasons other than taste? Licking is often part of kissing. It is the centerpiece of oral sex. How can we experience the pleasure of licking without the SAS blaring, "Watch OUT!" For many women licking is something done to them, to their vaginas, their breasts. Some women find it pleasurable and others do not. Doing the licking for heterosexual women primarily means licking and sucking the penis, something challenging for many women. Some hate it, some tolerate it as a way to give him pleasure or to get off the hook, and some love it. Women don't get lessons on how to lick sexually. At least if a woman has a woman partner, she is licking places she knows something about. A penis is not so familiar and may well be scary.

Goal: To find some positive experiences associated with licking starting with those associated with taste.

Preparation: First get the necessary items for this exercise (see below). Sit some place private and relaxing and put your items on a table next to you.

Directions:

1. Pour something you like onto a plate, for example, maple syrup, strawberry juice, or chocolate. Slowly lick it off feeling the sensations on your tongue. Feel the delight and surprise of the taste plus any other sensations such as tingling.
2. Find something that you can lick up and down and all around, for example an ice cream bar, a cherry, a plum. Experience the texture, the temperature, the tingling, and any other sensations you might have.
3. Now put something on your arm and lick it off. After it is gone, just lick your arm. Notice the feel of your skin on your tongue and the feel of your tongue on your skin.

Tingling/Electric Sensations

During sex, tingling sensations can occur at various times. For example, as arousal grows and spreads, women can feel delightful tingling in their fingers and toes. Particularly at their most erotic areas they may experience tingling or electric sensations. What are these experiences? Tingling is a light sensation of dancing energy in a woman's body. It is an on and off experience like a flickering light. Electric sensations are more intense feelings of streaks shooting from one place in the body to another. They wake a woman up and grab her attention. They are most pleasant and enlivening. To help a woman client experience these sensations without arousal, you can suggest the following exercises.

Goal: To create a tingling/electric sensation on your skin.

Preparation: Sit in a relaxing place in a comfortable chair.

Directions:

1. Lightly touch your skin with your fingernails in a sensitive place such as your inner forearm, your inner upper arm, or your inner thighs. Slowly and gently draw your nails up and down your skin. This can create goose bumps.
2. Shake your hands out as if there is something sticky on them that you want to get off. Yuck! Really fling those hands around. Then stop, close your eyes, and feel the tingling energy coursing through your hands.

3. Our bodies have certain spots on them that are quite sensitive. When touched, these spots can feel releasing, electric, or a "hurts so good" sensation. You may have discovered some of these sensations being massaged. Common places to find these points are at the base of the neck, in the middle of your buttock cheek and in the jaw muscle. Explore around in areas that you can reach for some of these points. Find one that creates an electric wave radiating out to areas of your body.

Spreading

Spreading involves taking a sensation in your body and moving it to another part of your body with your hands. When the sensation spreads, it grows, it includes more of your body, and you feel more full. When you discover that you can actually make sensations move into more of your body, you can feel amazed and empowered.

Goal: To move warmth from your chest down into your belly and to learn how to spread energy in your body.

Preparation: Sit in a comfortable chair or lie on your bed in a relaxing setting.

Directions: Start with some Simple Breathing to create energy in your chest. Start with placing your palms on your chest. Slowly move your hands straight down over your diaphragm to your belly. Then bring your palms around to the side of your pelvis and back up the sides of your chest to where you started. Now add in the Simple Breathing to create energy in your chest. Then using the hand movements, spread the energy through your chest and belly. Another place you can try spreading is on your face. Massage your forehead with your fingers. As your feel some letting go and relaxing in your forehead, bring your hand down to your cheeks, spreading the relaxed feeling.

Anita felt numb in many parts of her body. There were only a few places where she could feel sensations. We determined that her SAS was working overtime and had shut her down. With the breathing exercises she could feel an opening and expanding in her chest. She also had quite sensitive hands. I gave her the homework to do the Simple Breathing exercise. Once she felt her chest area open up, I suggested she take one hand and imagine spreading the sensations in her chest down into her diaphragm and belly. Slowly she was able to experience the energy moving. Thrilled to be able to broaden her sensations, she went on to spreading her sensations into other parts of her body, amazed at what was possible. Gradually she was able to feel sensations traveling down from her chest into her arms and hands.

Expanding

Expanding involves a gradual opening of a woman's whole body. It is the result of spreading and filling out. Thus, it is bigger than spreading, which involves moving sensations out from one part of the body to another. Expanding is growing, becoming larger and fuller. It is fulfilling, exciting, sometimes even a bit scary as a woman's capacity grows. It is part of the sexual experience in a number of ways. Physically blood flows into new areas and fills those areas so they expand. The vulva grows larger. A woman's breathing becomes fuller and expands the chest, abdomen, and pelvis. Arousal increases her sexual sensations, which can be frightening because it may be unfamiliar or feel out of control. Being able to feel the sensations of expansion without arousal can help a woman become more comfortable with the experience of extending outward. Below are some expanding exercises for your women clients.

Goal: To create and experience the sensation of expanding your body.
Preparation: #1 and #2: sit up in a comfortable chair in a relaxed setting.
#3: Lie on your bed in a comfortable environment.
Directions:

1. Try the Simple Breathing exercise described above. Focus on the sensations of your diaphragm, chest, and pelvis expanding. Feel more air coming into you. Feel your muscles and skin as they stretch outward.
2. Repeat the Simple Breathing exercise, this time adding expansion of your arms. Fold your arms over your chest. As you inhale, open them up and stretch them out to the sides fully. As you exhale, bring them in again to the folded position. Let yourself experience this filling up and releasing.
3. Lying on your bed, curl up into a ball on your side. Gradually unfold, rolling onto your back and stretching out your legs followed by your arms until you are fully open. Then gradually go back into the curled up position. Slowly continue to go back and forth into curled and uncurled positions. Feel the contrast of opening and expanding, then closing and curling back up. Feel the safety of the curled position and the freeness of the open position. Be aware of any discomfort in either position or in the transition between the two.

Rocking

Rocking involves a clear movement back and forth. It is both stimulating and soothing. It is rhythmic and pulsating. We seem to like the rocking motion. We even have chairs specially made to rock back and forth. During the sexual experience, people often do various rocking motions primarily with their pelvises. Why do people rock during sex? It gives more sensation, it creates more contact between bodies, and it creates more friction. Plus it is more fun. People rock their bodies during masturbation as well as during partner sex. Here are some rocking exercises to suggest for opening up.

Goal: To learn to rock your body and to open it up to more sensations.
Preparation: #1: Sit upright in a slightly cushioned chair in a relaxing setting.
#2 and #3: Stand up and bend your knees slightly.
#4: Sit on a carpeted floor or on a mat.
Directions:

1. Sitting in a chair, rock your pelvis back and forth. Feel the movement on your buttocks as you rock. Close your eyes and let the rhythm move through your whole body. Feel both the soothing and the pulsing aspects of the movement.
2. Standing up, rock your pelvis back and forth. To do this, bring your genitals under and forward while your waist goes in and down. Then reverse and push your buttocks out and back while you bring your waist forward and out. Gently rock back and forth feeling the movement. Then try different speeds and rhythms.
3. Rock just your upper body from the waist up. Push your chest forward and then back from your waist.
4. Sitting on a carpet or a mat, bring your knees up to your chest and hold them with your arms. Then slowly rock backward onto your back. Then, using the momentum, reverse direction rocking back up into a sitting position. Repeat this back and forth movement feeling the rhythm and the flow. Feel yourself to be like a pendulum swinging back and forth. If you have a problem with your back, it is probably best not to try this particular exercise.

Sliding and Gliding

Sliding is a continuous movement across a surface. Two surfaces make contact, creating friction and sensation. Snakes slide, sleds slide, doors slide, skiers and skaters slide and glide. Gliding implies a long, flowing continuous movement. Going downward makes sliding and gliding faster. Going upward or across requires force to move. In being physically intimate partners slide and glide in various ways. In caressing they slide their hands across each other's bodies. One partner can also slide her body across the other partner's body. In kissing partners slide their lips around on each other's lips. In intercourse a man slides his penis back and forth inside a woman's vagina. In masturbation women slide their own hands over their vulvas, clitorises, and breasts. There are things women can use to help sliding such as moisture, creams, and lubrication. Here are some sliding exercises to suggest for your woman client:

Goal: To experience the sensations of various ways of sliding and gliding with your body.

1. *Preparation:* Lie on your bed in a warm room preferably on sheets with a silky or satiny finish.

   Directions: Slide your body around on the sheets using the muscles of your legs, buttocks, and back. Feel the contact of the sheets on your body and feel the stimulation of your skin.

2. *Preparation:* Lie on your front on your bed.

   Directions: Slide yourself again on the bed feeling your belly and your breasts on the sheets. Try moving at different speeds. Feel the sensations on your front where your skin may be particularly sensitive.

3. *Preparation:* Find various soft fabrics such as suede, velvet, velour, silk, etc., to slide over your body on your skin.

   Directions: Start on your arms, then move to your chest and breasts. Glide the fabrics over your body sensing the different textures and feeling your skin respond to the different fabrics. Pick your favorite and notice why you particularly like the feeling it gives you. Let yourself absorb the experience.

4. *Preparation:* Find a comfortable couch or adjustable chair with a soft fabric covering.

   Directions: With little or no clothing slide around on the chair or couch in different ways. For example, sink and slide down the back of the chair feeling the movement and fabric on your skin.

5. *Preparation:* Sit in a comfortable chair in a relaxed atmosphere.

   Directions: If you have ever skied or skated, close your eyes and take yourself back to the sensations of moving smoothly across the snow or ice. Feel the length of your movement being carried forward from the initial effort, now gliding and sailing along. Feel the letting go into the movement.

Crystal could not get herself to glide or slide on her bed. It seemed stupid and forced. We then went back to childhood images of her gliding or sliding. She remembered sledding down a special hill in the winter. Each year in his back yard the father of a neighborhood friend would build a wonderful slide track with curves and turns. The kids were waiting with anticipation for that first moment of exhilaration heading down the hill and around the turns. This image connected Crystal with the feeling of continuous movement and body release. She resolved to take her kids sledding to feel that movement once again. Meanwhile she was now able to take in and enjoy the body sensations as she practiced sliding on her bed.

Rolling

Rolling is so freeing! Remember the feeling of rolling down a hill as a child? Slowly rolling, then gathering momentum? As adults this might be overwhelming: that feeling of letting go, whirring. As adults we roll slowly, perhaps in bed when we turn over. During sex with a partner, we may roll around each other when changing positions. Think how intrigued we are with rolling. We love to watch gymnasts and clowns roll in amazing ways. Suggest to a woman client that she try rolling a little at a time to prevent dizziness and fear.

> *Goal:* To experience the flow of rolling movement in your body.
> *Preparation:* #1, #2, #4: Lie on your bed.
> #3: Stand up.
> *Directions:*

1. On your bed slowly roll your head side to side feeling each little spot on the back of your head as you turn. Imagine your whole body is rolling with you.
2. Roll your arms, then your legs back and forth feeling the circular motion. Then rotate your wrists and then ankles.
3. Standing up, roll your hips around in a circle. Feel the fluidity of the movement.
4. Now try rolling your whole body over on the bed. Feel the deliciousness of falling over and being caught.

Anna could not relate to rolling, but she was intrigued by the idea. We brainstormed, looking for times when she might have rolled and really felt the movement. She had no memories of rolling down hills or rolling in bed. I asked her to imagine being various things that roll, for example, a ball, a rolling pin, a log. Rolling the dough! She could remember the feeling of rolling up dough with her hands to make cookies and pastries. So I suggested she be the dough and imagine being rolled. We went through some relaxation exercises that she could use to let go and become soft. At home she lay on the floor and imagined being the dough being pushed across a counter. After a few tries, she was able to feel floppy, loose, and rolled around. Then we were able to carry this feeling into other ways of her rolling her body.

Thrusting

Thrusting is a back and forth movement with a push forward and then a retraction. The retraction is a rebound movement and a preparation for the next push. The push is to create contact and impact. We usually thrust to move into, out of, and then into again. We can thrust our tongues in and out of our mouths. We thrust our legs down and back around pushing against the air to bicycle. When we swim, we thrust our arms forward in the crawl and then back under to return.

Many women think of intercourse when they think of thrusting. In fact, thrusting may have a negative feeling for women. It is what is done to them. Male partners may not be sensitive to how thrusting during intercourse feels to a woman. Men do not have a vulnerable soft moist vagina into which a hard pushing penis thrusts forward. For women thrusting may be associated with what the man wants or with his force. But, women can thrust too. In the sexual experience a woman can thrust her pelvis up and down or back and forth over a male partner's penis or just against her partner's body creating sensations. Learning thrusting movements can be a way for a woman to take charge and allow herself to be aggressive. Thrusting can also be gentle. These exercises are for women to experience thrusting without arousal.

Goal: To feel the push and pull of thrusting in your body.
Preparation: Stand in a comfortable relaxed position in a relaxed setting.
Directions:

1. Imagine yourself as a wave on a beach. Waves thrust forward and then retreat only to return. Imagine gentle waves and feel your body to be those waves. Push your chest forward and then pull it back, inhaling as you go forward and exhaling as you pull back. Breathing is a form of thrusting.
2. Thrust your pelvis forward and back, feeling first the push of it and then the pulling back, getting ready to move forward again. As you continue this movement, feel the rhythm and the energy of the move-ment.

Feeling Out of Control

One of the most compelling and scary aspects of sexual experience is feeling out of control. We are both drawn to and repelled by out of control experiences. Thus, we seek out things like zip lines, roller coasters, alcohol. At the same time we avoid out of control experiences such as getting lost and getting dizzy. We are certainly ambivalent about losing control. When we are sexually aroused at a heightened level and when we have an orgasm, we lose a sense of space and time. One of the most delicious aspects of sexual experience is how completely absorbing and powerful it can be. Our body sensations take over. We lose our minds and we give into immediate intense sensations. How wonderful and how terrifying! It is particularly scary if it feels foreign, sinful, wrong, unwanted, and/or forced upon us. If this is an experience that a woman wasn't supposed to have or didn't choose to have, the out of control feelings can be overwhelming and terrifying. Heiman and LoPiccolo (1988) describe women's fear of loss of sexual control. "Some women . . . are afraid that if they let themselves feel sexual desire, they will be unable to control themselves. They fear they will become immoral, insatiable, and wanton if they let any of their sexual drive out, so they automatically turn off" (p. 161).

When women enjoy out of control sensations, they can lead to quite amazing experiences of releasing, escaping, transcending, and heightened pleasure described later in the book as Surrendering. These experiences can take women to a new level where they find their inner spirit and connection to a greater energy. The following two exercises introduce women to out of control feelings. Suggest them when your client is ready.

Goal: To introduce out of control feelings separate from sex, controllable by you and potentially enjoyable.
Preparation: Sit or stand in a comfortable position in a relaxed setting.
Directions:

1. Shake your head up and down, side to side, back and forth, and around. Our heads are the locus of our control. Letting them go can clear our brains and introduce the physical sense of release. Do this exercise gently at first and only if your health allows it.
2. Sounds: Begin with the sound exercises suggested earlier. After getting used to making sounds, practice some real releasing sounds such as yelping, screaming, and howling. In order not to alarm anyone or inhibit yourself, you can make these sounds in your car, in your basement (if you have one) when no one is home, and/or with your face in a pillow to muffle the sound. When making these sounds, draw them up from deep within so that you can feel them and not hurt your throat.

Vibrating/ Jiggling

Vibrating involves continuous short, quick, back and forth movements that create frequencies. Vibrating is essential to many parts of our lives. It occurs everywhere. We vibrate as we breathe, as our heart pumps, and as our blood vessels pulsate. Vibrating is what allows instruments to make sound. Our vibrating vocal cords allow us to make sounds, all kinds of sounds. Without vibrating there would be no sound. Vibrating is energy. It is glorious! We talk about a person being vibrant, meaning that they are alive and glowing. When we are sexual, we vibrate. Often parts of our bodies move back and forth in short rhythmic movements.

During orgasms women vibrate in various ways. Their vaginas and uteruses, for example, contract rhythmically in vibrating motions. Vibrating helps women release and let go of control. Learning to vibrate voluntarily can teach them to be in tune, to sense, to wake up, and to prepare for more sensation in the sexual experience. Musicians understand the experience of vibrations passing through their bodies. Many of us have purposely vibrated to stay warm. We shiver, quickly moving at short intervals back and forth. Jiggling is basically vibrating, but it implies a more purposeful movement. Soft tissues jiggle best. To jiggle or vibrate, women can move parts of their bodies on their own or they can use one part to move another. Here are some exercises to help women learn to jiggle and vibrate.

Goal: To experience the rhythmic releasing and life-giving sensations of vibrating and jiggling.
Preparation: #1, #2, and #3: Sit or lie on your bed.
#4 and #5: Stand on the floor.
Directions:

1. Sit on your bed and place your hands on your thighs. Now vibrate your thighs with your hands. Jiggle them back and forth in opposite directions, in other words, pushing both thighs in together and out together. Do this at various paces. Feel the energy in your thighs as you do this.
2. Lying down now jiggle both legs on their own, in and out together. Feel the movement and the awakening of your energy.
3. Roll onto the right side of your body. Take your left hand and jiggle your left buttock. Give it a good strong jiggle. Now turn to the other side and repeat this. Feel the pleasure of the sensations flowing through your pelvis.

4. Stand up and try shimmying, moving your shoulders back and forth and jiggling your breasts. Try this with your bra on and then off to see the different sensations. Move slowly and then try different speeds. Notice the sensation of your breasts and chest moving.

5. Stand on the floor. Imagine that the floor is vibrating. Begin to vibrate your legs back and forth. Feel the vibrations and energy move through your legs into your buttocks. Now let the vibrations move into your whole pelvis. Feel them pulsating upward. Step by step let the vibrating spread into your upper body: your chest, your back, your arms, your shoulders, and your head. Let the vibrations take over your whole body and stay with it for five to ten minutes. When you are done, stand and feel the energy that you have awakened. The next time that you do this, let the vibration go into your genitals. We usually forget the genitals.

Margo Anand (1989) describes an exercise she calls "The Streaming Process" (pp. 279–285). It is similar to the above vibration exercises and is designed to trigger a response of letting go and ecstasy in your body. She incorporates rocking, vibration, relaxation, and breathing. Vibrating can connect us with a greater energy beyond ourselves.

Maya had never connected vibrating with the idea of opening up her body. Yet, she was a singer and vibrating felt natural to her. She appreciated the role vibration played in releasing and expressing. Taking vibration into her whole body was more of a challenge than she expected. She wanted to start with the homework of whole body vibrating, but it felt forced. So, we backed off and began with her hands and arms. Once she was able to vibrate different parts of her body and feel the rhythm and intensity, she connected to the sensations and felt a wonderful letting go.

Shaking

Shaking is a quick movement that allows us to release energy as we also build energy. One of the great things about shaking is that there is no elegant or right way to do it. We are less likely to judge ourselves about how we shake than how we do some other movements. Shaking has a somewhat spastic quality to it. During sexual experiences, women may shake in various ways. Sometimes they shake to enhance sensation. For example, they can shake their legs in order to build arousal. They can shake their heads to lose themselves. During orgasm women often shake involuntarily. Thus, learning to shake can teach their bodies to experience more and to let go. Below are some fun shaking exercises to suggest to your women clients.

Goal: To learn to release and build energy in an easy and accessible way through Shaking.

Preparation: Stand in a relaxed location and put on some music with a good beat.

Directions:

1. Start by shaking just your hands. Imagine that you have something on them that is hard to get off. Start slowly and build up the motion. Stay with it for a minute or more. When you are done, stop, close your eyes, and feel the energy in your hands. You may feel warmth or tingling. The energy that you have created can be a pleasant surprise. This is an easy way to show yourself how you can create energy in your body. Imagine where you could go from here.

2. Shake your pelvis by moving it from side to side. To do this, use your leg and buttock muscles bending one knee and then the other. As you bend one knee, let that hip lower while the other hip rises. Then reverse this motion. Start slowly and then gradually move more rapidly. Imagine you are releasing restrictions and shaking off inhibitions. You can also shake your pelvis moving it forward and back.

3. Try shaking out other parts of your body, for example, your head and your shoulders. Find parts that feel good to shake.

Margo Anand (1989) describes a similar shaking exercise in her book *The Art of Sexual Ecstasy.* She calls it "Shaking Loose" (pp. 276–279).

Total Body Shaking

This is an exercise that allows a woman to let go of control. It is difficult to stay in control when you are shaking out your whole body for a period of time to music with a good strong beat. This exercise is a prime one for experiencing Surrendering (see next chapter) and for connecting to one's inner spirit.

Goal: To totally let go into a full body release through Shaking.

Preparation: Stand up in a relaxing space that is large enough to not worry about hitting or banging into something. Put on some music with an intense and strong beat, preferably a beat that increases in speed as it plays.

Directions: Begin with shaking your hands as described above. Gradually add other parts of your body. First flap your arms and flail them about. Then add your head, letting it shake up and down, side to side. Then add your shoulders moving them up and down, forward and back, alternately and together. Then shake your whole upper body from your waist up. Let your body sway and shake. Then add your pelvis with quick "shake your booty" movements. Then add your legs shaking, jumping, and kicking. Throughout let out sounds beginning softly and eventually adding bird noises, whooping, roaring, or whatever wants to come out. Feel the release of energy. Let yourself dissolve into the movement. Lose yourself in the letting go. This is your time to feel your whole body discharging, expressing, and opening!

Boys would walk by Claudia and cluck and make circular movements with their hands. They were imitating touching her large breasts. Try as she did to disguise them with bulky draping clothes, they stood out there announcing themselves, so it seemed, to all the boys in her middle school. She had a reputation, one that did not fit her at all. Finally as an adult she had breast reduction surgery and started a new life. No longer were her breasts the butt of jokes and stares. Yet, she kept her body as still as possible, afraid to move lest her breasts jiggle too much. She couldn't imagine being able to move well. Taking a dance class as an adult helped her feel better about her body. Yet, during sex, she would try to not move much. When I first told her about the Total Body Shaking exercise, she turned pale. We needed to work through her fears and old feelings. Gradually she was willing to try some shaking with her hands and arms. What a triumph it was for her when, on her own, she was finally able to let her whole body, including her breasts, just let loose and shake! Because of the formlessness of the shaking, she was able to let go and let the movement take over her body.

Undulating and Writhing

Writhing involves undulating movements. An impulse travels up the body in successive ripples. Think of an ostrich's neck as it walks. The bottom part moves and passes the movement up the neck. Writhing involves parts of the body moving in different directions in a smooth way. The hips push out to the left as the chest moves to the right and the head to the left. Then the movement reverses, coming back and moving in the opposite direction: hips to the right, chest to the left, and head to the right. It may work better for a woman to not think about the movements and just do whatever undulating and writhing means to her. During the sexual experience, people often undulate and writhe. These movements are enhancing, inviting, and seductive. They say, "Come join me. I am lost in sensation and pleasure."

Goal: To feel the sensuality of undulating and writhing movement pulsating in your body.

Preparation: Lie on your bed and play some sensuous music. Some good music with undulating rhythms and drums will help the body to respond. Flute music and Middle Eastern music are great.
Directions:

1. Start with just your arms. Try using your joints as pivots to move parts of your arms in different directions: move your elbow into your body and your wrist away with your bent hand following your wrists, then reverse. Then move both your arms in mirror images of each other doing this undulating movement. Finally allow time to writhe your arms in any old way that you want.
2. Lying down on your back imagine that you are bicycling on a flat plane. Bend one knee and draw your heel up toward you across the bed. Then straighten your leg as you move the other knee toward you in the same manner. Let your hips swivel as you make these movements.
3. Lie down and feel an impulse go through your body, beginning at your feet and legs and moving up your body. Let the music guide the impulses as they ripple through you. Then let yourself writhe in any way you feel.

Janina laughed as she described trying undulating and writhing at home on her bed. She loved the feeling of it and felt a bit foolish at the same time. We worked on images that would help her feel the movement more. She giggled at the thought of being an ostrich walking with its neck undulating forward and back. Sitting in my office she played with imagining herself as an ostrich. At home she laughed a lot as she walked around the house acting like the big bird. She even had her nine-year-old daughter join in. Together they strode around undulating and feeling quite regal. Fun can be an important part of these exercises.

Thrashing

Thrashing is a vigorous high-energy movement of the body going side to side, back and forth, and all around. Legs and arms move quickly this way and that. The trunk of the body may roll, rock, and thrust all mixed together. Little kids thrash about to express frustration, fun, and a desire to get loose. During sex adults often thrash at the height of excitement, expressing the rush of sexual energy through their bodies. They may particularly thrash during orgasm as the orgasm takes over the body with an outburst. (Note that there are many kinds of orgasms, some of which are gentler and quieter.) Orgasm is a time of letting go of control, getting lost in the sensation.

Thrashing is both an expression of this reaction and an enhancement of it, helping the experience to become heightened and longer. We want to prolong the ecstasy.

Practicing thrashing is a great way to experience releasing because it is hard to stay in control when thrashing. For women who have trouble letting go, Thrashing, like Shaking, can give them a taste of the experience of releasing. It may be a challenge for women to actually let themselves thrash if they are not used to it. Have your woman client begin these exercises gradually.

Goal: To gradually surrender into the kicking and flailing movements of Thrashing using your whole body.
Preparation: Lie on your bed in a comfortable quiet environment.
Directions:

1. Lie on a bed and first practice earlier movements such as Rolling and Rocking. When you are comfortable with these movements, add an element of uncoordinated movement. Roll, then fall side to side with some gentle kicking of your legs and flailing of your arms. Feel what it is like to be more open and a bit wild.
2. Now increase the speed of your movements, adding more Thrashing movements like kicking and flailing. Let the movements become wider and fuller. Begin to let some sounds out.
3. Lie on the bed and practice having a temper tantrum on your back. Build it up gradually. Raise your arms up and down, first one arm and then the other hitting the bed. Kick your legs up and down with your knees slightly bent. Add rolling your head from side to side. Let out some good yells as you gradually increase the speed and intensity of the movements. Let yourself get to a point where you lose yourself in the movement and you let out some good loud sounds. Feel the joy of abandon.

SUMMARY

Now a whole menu of possibilities has been opened to your women clients: Breathing, Rolling, Licking, Vibrating, etc. These are the movements of the sexual experience without the arousal. It may amaze you how many movements there are and how varied they are. Now, how do you know what to suggest in what order? Chapter 12 shows a progression of exercises that include the Ingredients and that go step by step in a way to give women safety and guidance.

Chapter Twelve

The Progressive Exercises

Establishing safety is a key element for women in dealing with their Sexual Alarm System. Women need to move in a slow progression that helps them be able to open up with care. The Progressive Exercises Program is comprised of four successive stages that take a woman through Awakening, Awareness, Allowing, and Surrender. At each stage exercises from the Ingredients section that fit the stage are included. Summaries of these Ingredients exercises are given. Other additional exercises from other sources of movement such as yoga, Tantra, dancing, and daily life experience are then added to the stage to expand the options from which to choose. Each new exercise is presented with the goal, preparation, and directions to make the exercises accessible and clear. Each is written as directions to your client from you, the therapist. Finally several groups of exercises are described. Each group consists of an exercise chosen from each of the four Progressive Exercises such that the exercises flow together from one step to the next.

The Progressive Exercises help a woman move thorough several of the Four Steps of Sexual Healing described in chapter 1. They not only focus on establishing safety, they also help women own their own female sexuality and begin very carefully to expand their sexuality by themselves.

As you help your women clients move through the four Progressive Exercises stages, choose those exercises that fit with where each woman is in her journey and that she can physically do without discomfort.

AWAKENING

To undo the withdrawing and shutting down effects of the SAS, women need to first awaken their bodies. There are soft, subtle ways of Awakening and more quick, energized ways of Awakening. Awakening can be delicious, shocking, and/or relieving. Women may resist it because it opens up the pain they have pushed under. They may feel too vulnerable. It is important to do these exercises in the context of safety and support. As a therapist, you play an important role in helping your women clients to feel safe enough to try these exercises.

Exercises from the Ingredients Section

Breathing Exercises

Breathing awakens us. It is an essential element of feeling our bodies. When many of us go to hug a person, we hold our breath. Why? So we don't feel our bodies pressed into another person and so the other person doesn't really feel us either. Breathing is living. Our breath is the essence of being alive and feeling. In Tantric approaches to sexuality, breathing is a central part of the philosophy and the exercises. We find this also in many spiritual approaches to the body, for example, yoga and the martial arts. When we are in high alert and sexual shutdown mode, our breathing becomes shallow and minimal. We need our energy for other essential protective actions. To open up our breathing there are soft techniques and energized techniques. For soft breathing techniques see Simple Breathing and Genital Breathing in the above Ingredients section. These are summarized below as directions to give your client. For energized breathing, see the Breath of Fire exercise.

1. Simple Breathing: The basic in and out of the breath brings new energy into your body. It awakens you and lets you know that you are a living being capable of sensation in your body.
2. Genital Breathing: As a woman, your genitals are often asleep and therefore seemingly nonexistent. Breathing in and out through your genitals awakens you to the possibility of having sensations in this forgotten area.

Other Ingredients Exercises to Awaken a Woman

1. Sounds: Soft sounds can gently enliven you as you feel and hear them. "Ahhh" is a sound that reminds you that you are here and helps you to let go. Try other vowel sounds such as "Ohhh" and "Eeee."

2. Vibrating: Review the directions for different ways of beginning the Vibrating exercises in the previous chapter. Putting your hand on different parts of your body and gently vibrating them brings energy into your body, reviving you.
3. Tingling: Try some of the Tingling exercises, particularly the first one where you lightly draw your fingernails across your skin, waking you up and possibly giving you goose bumps.

Additional Awareness Exercises

Below are more exercises that awaken women. They bring in strong breathing and quick movement. Before doing any of the exercises, assess with your woman client what she can do without hurting herself. Most of the exercises are nonstrenuous. Many are simple and familiar.

1. The Fall Over

Goal: To awaken your body with a deep breath and a quick energizing movement.
Preparation: Stand up tall in a comfortable environment.
Directions: Slowly raise your arms over your head in the following way. Take a deep inhale as you raise your arms out to the side and up next to your head. Hold your breath and feel the gathered energy inside of you. Keeping your legs standing with a slight bend in the knees, let your upper body fall over from the waist, emitting a full exhale with sound. Shake out your upper body in this half-hanging position. Let yourself feel the energy you have generated.

In my Body Work for Sexual Health and Healing workshop, after introductions, I would begin the exercise part of the day with this Fall Over exercise. Suddenly the room would come alive as the women's bodies came awake. Inhaling, exhaling, swaying, shaking out! Eyes would open more widely. Arms and legs were moving. Energy was generated. This is a great exercise for women to become alert and aware that they have a body that can respond and feel.

2. Jumping exercise

Goal: To awaken your body with intense movements.
Preparation: Stand up in a comfortable environment with space around you.
Directions: Jump up and down and shake your body all over as you let out sounds.

3. Body Slap

Goal: To jump start your body into sensation.
Preparation: Stand up in a comfortable environment.
Directions: Use your hands to gently and firmly slap your body first on your thighs, then down your calves. Then go up your body on your buttocks, chest, shoulders, and neck. Feel the Awakening with the strong sensations on your skin.

AWARENESS

After Awakening, we need to become aware of what we have awakened. Awareness requires consciousness and focus. To do this, we may have to move through some unpleasant feelings such as fear and anger. Wendy Maltz (1991) describes developing "Active awareness" (p. 256) which she defines as including body movements, thoughts, and emotions with the goal of helping "you feel conscious, safe and in control" (p. 256). Awareness is the cornerstone of the practice of mindfulness described by many authors such as Jon Kabat-Zinn (2005).

Awareness Exercises from the Ingredients Section

For each of these movements refer back to the Ingredients section for the full directions. Below is a reminder of each movement.

1. A number of exercises from Awakening can be used also to develop Awareness by taking them deeper and staying focused on your sensations. For example, the Simple Breathing can be further developed by staying focused on your inhaling and exhaling. Let yourself become aware of what is happening inside your body. Feel as your muscles let go and tension releases. Panting greatly increases Awareness of your whole chest, diaphragm, and belly area as well as your head and face.
2. The Pelvic Rock both awakens energy and provides an opportunity for focusing on the energy as it comes into and goes out of your body. You can become aware of your pelvis in a new way, feeling sensations in your belly and buttocks.
3. Receiving Touch: This is a wonderful exercise for developing your awareness of different sensations on your skin.
4. Making Faces: Much of the time we are unaware of what our face is doing. This exercise draws our attention to our expressions and how they feel as we make them.

Additional Awareness Exercises

1. The Butterfly

Goal: This yoga position is often used for stretching the inner thighs and lower pelvic area. You can add a breathing component to increase your awareness of your body experience.

Preparation: Lie on the floor on your back on a rug or a mat in a comfortable environment.

Directions: Bring your knees up, keeping your feet on the floor. Then let each knee fall gently to the outside such that the bottoms of your feet are facing each other. An alternate position is to lie in the same position, but up against a wall. That is, your buttocks are tucked up against the floor and wall and your open legs are up and supported by the wall. Your knees are open and your feet are resting facing each other with the outside of each foot against the wall. To add the breathing, inhale while you open your vulva and vagina, imagining that you are drawing air directly into your vagina. Then exhale as you contract your vagina, imagining that you are blowing the air out of your vagina. Feel the energy come into your genitals and your pelvis.

2. The Love Spot

In a number of Eastern approaches to sexual opening, there is a spot in the middle of your chest near your heart called the Love Spot. It is a center of heart energy that can connect to your sexual energy.

Ramsdale and Ramsdale (1991) describe the following: "the Love Spot is really more like a Love Cave. Here is the core of our ability to deeply feel" (p. 37).

Goal: To awaken loving energy within you.

Preparation: Sit upright in a comfortable chair in soft surroundings.

Directions: Put your hand on the Love Spot. Breathe in and out using Simple Breathing. Feel the energy of love and connection available to you from within. Become aware of the life force energy within you. In Eastern approaches life energy, creative energy, and sexual energy are all the same energy.

Irina started with the Simple Breathing to become more aware of her body. Feeling her chest to be alive, she put her hand on her Love Spot to give herself some caring. She found this exercise to be particularly calming. Never had she imagined that she could give this inner quiet to herself. She asked if she could stay with this exercise for some time. Of course! What a gift to herself.

3. Acupressure points
There are three points on the pubic mound that can awaken sexual energy. The first spot is right on the top and middle of the pelvic mound bone. The second spot is directly to the left and the third spot is directly to the right of this center spot both a half finger width away from the center and still on the bone (Reed Gach, 1997, p. 156).

> *Goal:* The goal is not to stimulate sexual arousal. It is to bring awareness to the possibility of sexual openness in your body.
> *Preparation:* Lie on your bed and first locate the three acupressure spots with your index finger.
> *Directions:* Take your index finger and gently press on the center spot. Then rotate your finger in a circle keeping it on the spot. This stimulates energy in the acupressure point. Do the same with one index finger on the left spot and the other on the right spot. Be aware of the energy you are opening and releasing.
> Just breathe into it.

ALLOWING

Now that your woman client has gained more aware of her sensations, she is ready to try exercises that allow those experiences to move and develop. Allowing exercises involve more movement through the body. Sensations are allowed to spread and grow inside of the woman, opening her up and expanding her.

Exercises from the Ingredients Section

For each of these movements refer back to the Ingredients section for the full directions. Below is a reminder of each movement.

1. Rolling is a wonderful exercise for experiencing movement as it unfolds in a continuous and moving way. Try first rolling your arm and then legs as suggested in the Ingredients section. Move on to rolling your whole body, allowing yourself to feel the letting go and the rhythm.

2. Sliding and Gliding are also exercises that allow sensations to unfold and grow. As parts of your body move along a surface, feel the subtle shifts in sensation. Feel the increase of sensitivity as the movement continues. It is delicious.

3. Rocking allows your body to feel momentum build and then shift. It is rhythmic and soothing as well as stimulating. Feel the expanding of your experience as the rocking goes back and forth.

4. Licking stimulates and allows sensation to spread across the tongue. Feel your tongue as it moves across your skin and feel your skin as it experiences your tongue.

5. Spreading moves energy from one part of your body to another, allowing sensation to expand and fill up more of your body.

6. Vibrating is a great exercise for Awareness and for Allowing. Once Vibrating different parts of your body opens up your Awareness, Allow the sensations to develop and move throughout your body.

Additional Allowing Exercises

1. T'ai Chi arms

Goal: T'ai Chi Ch'uan (Muir, 2008) is a system of body movement for meditation and self-defense. The goal is to feel a flow of healing energy move through your body.

Preparation: The movements all stem from a stance in which the knees are slightly bent and the pelvis is lowered creating a firm base of strength.

Directions: In this position, feel your feet planted firmly on the ground. Begin to slowly rotate your pelvis and upper body slightly to one side and then the other keeping your arms still at your sides. Lead the movement with your pelvis, letting your upper body follow. Slowly let your arms swing out to the side following your pelvis as it moves. When you reach the end of your rotation to one side, let your arms naturally wrap around your pelvis with your leading arm in front and your following arm in back. Then turn the other direction and repeat. Keep this movement going in a gentle rhythm, feeling the flow of your pelvis and arms. Allow the movement to go through you, feeling a stream of energy as it circulates inside of you. This will take a number of repetitions to feel.

2. Scarves Flowing

Goal: To extend the experience of flowing movement through your body by moving the scarves.

Preparation: Find two fairly long scarves of equal size. In each hand hold one of the scarves by its end.

Directions: Start moving your arms in circles in opposite directions, one clockwise and one counterclockwise. Let one hand be moving toward your body while the other is moving away from your body. Feel the flowing of this movement extended through the scarves, letting the circulating movement flow into the rest of your body.

In my workshop Body Movement for Sexual Health and Healing I would hand out scarves for the above Allowing exercise. Before using the scarves, we would do some of the Rocking and/or Vibrating exercises. The scarves exercise is one of my favorites because it brings in a wonderful flow of energy to the women's movements. They can feel the air moving through their scarves as they swirl them around. They can feel the scarves as extensions of themselves, allowing them to create gracious and lovely movement. Doing this exercise with others adds to a visual flow and sense of being part of a larger flow of movement. If your client has a friend or child who can do this with her, I suggest you strongly recommend including them.

3. Willow Tree

Goal: Through imagery to allow movement to flow through your body.
Preparation: Put on some flowing music that helps you to sense a breeze.
Directions: Allow your arms to be the branches of a willow tree moving all around the trunk. Let the music guide your arm movements, feeling the music move through you like a breeze.

4. Bells

Goal: To experience the reverberation of bells in your body.
Preparation: Lie on your bed and put on some music of only bells. A recording of Tibetan bells works well.
Directions: Listen to the bells as they ring. Feel your body to be the bells. Each time a bell rings, let it reverberate through your body, allowing the sound and frequencies of the bell to guide slight soft movements in your body.

SURRENDERING

This is the time for a woman to let herself go and abandon herself to her experiences. She can enjoy the fullness and the freeness of letting her sensations take over her body. Surrendering is also a time to transcend our ordinary experience and to connect to an energy greater than ourselves. Your woman client will need careful guidance from you for these Surrendering exercises. Pick those that you and she think she is ready to experience.

Exercises from the Ingredients Section

For each of these movements refer back to the Ingredients section for the full directions. Below is a reminder of each movement.

1. Shaking is a wonderful way to let go because it is vigorous and releasing and there is no right way to do it. Follow the directions in the Ingredients section, moving through various stages of shaking and then coming to the Total Body Shaking. You can jump around, scream, and let it loose.
2. Undulating and Writhing are quite sensuous ways of feeling your body slinking and gyrating. Feel the fullness of the movements as you move this way and that.
3. Thrusting is an assertive and powerful way of pushing your body forward. Feel your energy in the motion.
4. Thrashing can be an intense total body movement. Feel the releasing and feel your emotions as you really let yourself go.

Additional Surrendering Exercises

Pelvic Bounce

This is an exercise from Bioenergetics, a form of psychotherapy that focuses on releasing blocked emotions through the body (Lowen, 1994).

Goal: To release energy and emotions from your pelvis.
Preparation: Lie on a well cushioned mat on the floor on your back.
Directions: Draw your knees up so that your feet are on the floor and your knees are bent. Gently lift your pelvis slightly by pressing up with your buttock muscles and your feet. Your body will be in a triangle shape with your pelvis and chest as one plane. Then gently drop your pelvis on the mat. Repeat this movement to get the feel of it. Next as you drop your pelvis say the word, "No." Keep lifting and dropping as you repeat, "No." Begin to do this more rapidly saying "No" more forcefully. Feel the impact of your pelvis as it contacts the mat and as you say, "No." Let yourself yell it out. Then rest for a few minutes as you absorb the release. Slowly then begin the exercise again, this time saying more softly the word, "Yes." Let yourself really absorb the "Yes" through your body. Let the "Yes" grow in fullness and sound. Feel its power.

Heiman and LoPiccolo (1988) describe two exercises that have some of the characteristics of the pelvic bounce, "the bouncing pelvis" and the "pelvic lift" (p.71).

The Pelvic Bounce exercise can bring out strong emotions of release. My client Rose joined the Body Work for Sexual Health and Healing workshop. When we came to the Pelvic Bounce, having led up to it through many of the Awakening, Awareness, and Allowing exercises, she was ready to howl. And howl she did as she roared out her "No" with a full voice encouraged by the sounds from other women. Her "No" was to all the sexual pressure she had felt from her partner Cassandra over the years as well as from partners before. After the workshop back in my office she shared how liberating her release through this exercise had been. We planned how she could continue to do the exercise at home. She was nervous neighbors would hear and/or that she would not be able to let go. So we broke the exercise into two parts and practiced just the "Nos" in my office. Then at home she tried the Pelvic Bounce. Gradually as she felt ready, she put the sounds and movement together in her basement with loud music to cover her noise. For several weeks she released a lot of anger and frustration. Then she moved on to the bounces with the "Yes," which gave her a sense of softness and strength.

EXERCISES THROUGH THE FOUR STAGES

After you have helped your woman client work on exercises from each of the four steps in the Progressive Exercises, then you can put together a group of four exercises one from each of the four stages. Pick four that naturally work together for her. Below are some series that I suggest your client can try. Each exercise flows into the next, maximizing her experience of opening her body and preparing it for adding in the arousal experience.

Example One

> Step one: Awakening: Simple Breathing
> Step two : Awareness: Self-Caressing (from Receiving Touch)
> Step three: Allowing: Gliding
> Step four: Surrendering: Undulating and Writhing

These four exercises have similar qualities: softness and continuous movement. Progressing through them builds up the amount of movement so that by the time your client comes to Undulating and Writhing, she has a foundation of similar types of less intense movements to help her experience of Writhing be more organic and fun. The Simple Breathing awakens her body, bringing life energy flowing through her. Self-Caressing carries this back and forth movement from inside her body to her outer body, bringing awareness to her skin. Then through Gliding she can allow that flow to move through her as she slides over her sheets, using larger movements and more of her body. She can then let the Gliding become Undulating and full Writhing, releasing herself into a wonderful sensual experience. How full this can become even without yet adding arousal!

Example Two

> Step one: Awakening: Fall Over
> Step two: Awareness: Pelvic Rock
> Step three: Allowing: Rocking
> Step four: Surrendering: Thrusting or Thrashing

Each of these movements involves pushing and releasing. Progressing through the movements builds up sensation with each exercise paving the way for the next. They build to a full releasing of letting go and abandon. In doing the Fall Over exercise, encourage your woman client to feel the pushing up of her arms and breathing followed by the release of breath and body. Once she has awakened her body with this full movement, guide her to go to the Pelvic Rock exercise. The Awakening from the falling over will help her feel the more subtle breathing and rocking of these movements. Then suggest she move into the full body Rocking, allowing herself to feel the pushing and releasing rhythm of the movements. Finally for Surrendering, suggest she begin with the Thrusting movements, feeling the intensity of the momentum, the force of her movement. This can be followed by all-out Thrashing, which involves all over back and forth movements. This sequence builds to a crescendo of abandon and intensity that can be exhilarating. Add some Sounds, such as some whoops and hollers, and she is flying.

Example Three

> Step one: Awakening: Body Slapping/Tapping
> Step two: Awareness: Receiving Touch, scratching
> Step three: Allowing: Vibrating
> Step four: Surrendering: Shaking

This sequence is more subtle than the last one, yet it also can get intense as it builds. The exercises are based on rhythmic back and forth movements with the forth and back being equal rather than a pushing and releasing as in the above sequence. Encourage your woman client to let the Body Slapping be a more gentle rhythmic tapping motion. The parts of her body that she taps will feel a subtle vibration that awakens her sensations. The next step involves moderate back and forth scratching to stimulate her skin and bring Awareness to her nerve endings all over. Vibrating gets her body moving, allowing sensations to spread all through her body. Shaking takes the movement to a new level of wider, fuller Surrendering movements. She can let the build up through the previous steps help her go all out, adding "ahh" sounds to broaden her sensations.

CASE STUDY: LATANYA

LaTanya came into therapy with two presenting issues: lack of sexual energy toward the man with whom she lived and a restricted sense of her own sexuality. She found her partner Donelle attractive, but she forgot about sexuality most of the time. What was wrong? Donelle was upset and baffled about how to approach LaTanya. After years of trying to turn her on, he had backed off much of the time. His approaches now were passive and not attractive to LaTanya.

LaTanya has a sense of drama about her that often draws male attention, something she both craves and fears. A full-bodied woman, she is tall and brunette with curly shoulder length hair. Wherever she goes, there is a flourish about her as if the wind has just blown in and swirled around the room. Her full long skirts enhance this impression. Yet, the frequent attention she receives from men also frightens her. Numerous times she has, in fact, been followed and approached in ways that unnerved her. Her SAS is often on alert. Underneath she believes that men are only interested in her for their sexual pleasure. She both plays into this belief to get attention and then shuts down when she gets it.

In her therapy we dealt with the SAS early on. Like many women she cried when I explained what the SAS is and how it works. She was overcome that her reaction was so universal. She had believed that something was wrong with just her.

LaTanya's first work was to develop her own sense of sexuality separate from her partner. We began with Awakening and Awareness exercises that she did at home. She needed to feel her body sensations as her own, slowly and non-sexually. Having taken yoga classes she was able to embrace both the Simple Breathing and the Pelvic Breathing to bring her body awake and to become aware of the energy moving through her. She felt joy and pride in sensing her body for herself and not for anyone else. We were off to a good start. The Simple Breathing awakened sensations in her chest and back. She focused on the sensations in these areas to develop more Awareness of her experience. The Pelvic Breathing awakened her whole pelvic area. Repeating the exercise brought more Awareness of the sensations of Tingling and warmth in this area.

When we moved into Allowing exercises, she had more difficulty. We began with the Spreading exercise. Using her hands to spread the energy from her breathing, she attempted to guide her energy from her chest and pelvis to her legs and arms. She could not feel much movement. Since some women respond better to some exercises than to others, I explain to them that there are many exercises to try until they find the one(s) that work for them. Given LaTanya's sense of flourish, I suspected that imagining herself as a willow tree might work for her. At home with music and the addition of scarves, she fell into the movement and allowed her self to sway and turn, dip and rise through her body. She loved it. We added gentle sounds to this movement to create more Allowing and flow. Whoosh! Eventually she moved into sliding movements on her bed. She felt inhibited and self-conscious at first. The motion eventually entranced her. For Surrendering, she chose to try Shaking and Thrashing. Both felt frightening in the beginning. She was not ready to let go of her guard even alone. Maintaining control and vigilance was extremely important. With reassurances that her SAS was not going to be disarmed by these experiences, she set out to try these exercises. She could tentatively do the Shaking, but stopped before a full out letting go. Thrashing on the bed seemed silly to her. We needed to do other work before she could surrender herself to these sensations.

For a period of time we addressed issues about her letting go. These were rooted in her family history of an alcoholic father who became sometimes flirtatious and sometimes angry when drinking. She and her siblings did not know which father would appear from day to day. Clearly LaTanya had chosen a husband who was more predictable and safe. There are times in doing this body work when other inhibiting issues need to be addressed before a woman can progress. LaTanya's work about her family dynamics was necessary before she could move forward into exercises that required Surrendering. Learning to identify and understand her issues and learning cognitive behavioral techniques to separate her past fears from today's reality, she was able to quiet her SAS enough to open herself to doing letting go exercises such as Thrashing and Writhing. In fact, she grew to thoroughly enjoy Undulating and Writhing to music. Through her work she also learned to need less attention from men and to feel and project more confidence.

SUMMARY

By now your woman client has experienced a number of exercises moving through the four Progressive Exercise steps: Awakening, Awareness, Allowing, and Surrender. Hopefully she has been able to combine some exercises from each step to experience a flow that is creating exciting new sensations.

Her sense of her body is changing and she feels new life and energy. When she feels ready, you can include her partner, if she has one, and share and expand her experiences. Chapter 13 adapts previous exercises for partners to do together.

IV

Beyond the Basic Experiences

Chapter Thirteen

Couples Exercises

Many of the exercises described above can be adapted for a woman to do with her partner. After she has worked with the Ingredients and the Progressive Exercises, she may be ready to bring some of the exercises to her relationship. If she does not have a partner, she can fantasize the following exercises together with an imagined loved one to help her be more receptive to an intimate relationship. In fact, even if she is in a partnership, it can be very helpful to imagine doing any one of these exercises with her partner before actually doing it. Imagining may help her to: 1) be more ready to do an exercise, 2) know better how she wants to do the exercise, and 3) know what she wants from her partner. The prime reason for bringing these exercises into her partnership is to help her turn off and transcend her SAS. By so doing she can open up her sexuality to a new level that is both safe and richly fulfilling beyond what she might have imagined.

To adapt the exercises to being in a couple, I go through the four stages of the Progressive Exercises describing how to use the ones that are most helpful and applicable for couples. Some of the exercises involve doing the activities side by side and some involve interacting together. The side by side ones are quite different for a woman when done with a partner rather than done by herself. Now the couple can share the experiences together, often changing how the woman herself experiences the exercise. For each exercise, guide the woman back to the Ingredients or Progressive Exercises chapters to refresh her about how to do the exercise.

The couples exercises work together with the Four Steps of Sexual Healing for a woman by establishing safety, setting limits with her partner, helping her to own her own female sexuality, and expanding her sexuality. This last step is particularly challenging being with a partner. It requires the first three steps to be well in place. It also requires trust and good communication between a woman and her partner. As the couple progresses through these exercises, guide the partners to choose those that appeal to them, are appropriate for them, and that they can physically do without discomfort.

AWAKENING

The goal of the couple Awakening exercises is for each partner to wake up to the other's presence. In the side by side exercises the partners are both awakening separately and gradually feeling each other's awakening. When one partner is helping the other to awaken, the energy and movement that partner is giving helps the other partner to come into his or her body and to feel alive. As the therapist, suggest the following exercises to your couple.

Breathing

1. Simple Breathing

Goal: To breathe together and be aware of each other's breathing.
Preparation: Sit together on a couch or on a bed in a relaxing setting.
Directions: Try doing the Simple Breathing exercise side by side. Feel the awakening of your body as your partner also awakens, creating a resonance and calmness between you.

2. Breath of Fire

Goal: To experience and feel each other's energy.
Preparation: Sit together on a bed in a relaxed setting.
Directions: See chapter 11 for directions. Doing this exercise side by side, like other side by side exercises, can be a "greater than two" experience. The energy that you each build sparks the other's energy and builds a greater energy together. You can build an aura of energy around the two of you by connecting to each other's energy. You do not need to be in synch to do the Breath of Fire. You can each go at your own pace.

Tapping

Goal: To experience physical contact in a loving way.
Preparation: Stand together in a comfortable place with space around you. The receiving partner either stands up or leans over from the waist with arms dangling toward the floor.

Directions: In the Progressive Exercises section, one of the exercises is Slapping to awaken your body. With a partner involved, I suggest you do gentle tapping in order to not set off the SAS. Very lovingly tap your partner on his/her back, legs, arms, and shoulders. Feel how the Tapping awakens the receiving partner's sensations and conveys caring and connection. Each partner has a turn as receiver.

Rebecca and Hannah liked the idea of the Tapping exercise. Both felt that it would help them make contact in a safe and caring way. First Hannah was the receiver and Rebecca was the tapper. Hannah bent over at the waist and took a few minutes to breathe deeply and shake out. She then signaled to Rebecca to begin. They struggled at first with Hannah giving too many directions and Rebecca getting annoyed. So they decided to start over with Rebecca as the receiver and Hannah as the giver. This worked better as Rebecca was able to receive and enjoy Hannah's all-over body tapping more easily. Being the giver first helped Hannah feel more in control and see how Rebecca could receive without giving constant directions. Then, as the receiver, Hannah was more able to relax.

Jumping Up and Down Together

Goal: To have some raucous fun.
Preparation: Stand together in a relaxing place with space around you.
Directions: Remember as a kid how you would jump up and down in excitement with your friends? It was like laughing: one starts and pretty soon others join in contagiously. So, imagine that you are kids and you are all excited about something that is going to happen. Decide together what that could be. One of you start jumping up and down being that excited kid. Then the other join in with laughter, shrieks, and jumping around.

AWARENESS

The couples Awareness exercises are designed to help each partner sustain attention and feel connected. They are meant to help the partners hold each other's presence inside of themselves and to share the awareness of that experience together. Below are Awareness exercises for you, as the therapist, to suggest to the couple. In some of the exercises, such as the second one, the directions are given for your woman client to be the giver and her partner to be the receiver. Discuss with your client who, in fact, should be the receiver and who should be the giver first. The order is flexible and may be important.

The Love Spot

Goal: This is a wonderful exercise for couples to bring awareness of each other's breathing and presence. Go back to the Progressive Exercises in chapter 12 to review the Love Spot exercise. Remember that the Love Spot is a place in the middle of your chest that goes through to your back. It is a center of love energy and sexual energy. This couples exercise is to help bring awareness of the love you feel for each other.
Preparation: Sit opposite each other in chairs in a comfortable environment.
Directions: Both close your eyes and breathe deeply, going inside of yourselves and calming yourselves. After a few minutes, each partner place your left hand on the other's heart. Feel each other's body rhythm. Try bringing your breathing in synch. If this is not comfortable, let it go. If it works, feel the inhale and exhale together being as one. Feel the connection between you, the connection of life energy and creative energy.

Yvonne and Derek found the Love Spot exercise quite special. They sat opposite each other, placed their left hands on each other's hearts and brought their breathing into synch. In doing this they were able to feel a connection between them that they hadn't felt in some time. As they recounted their experience, they smiled at each other and glowed. However, the second time they did the exercise, Derek became aroused and asked Yvonne to do oral sex to him. She resisted, reminding him that they weren't supposed to be sexual yet. He was not happy and neither was she. In the next therapy session I carefully explained how the point of the exercise was to relish the feelings they experienced the first time and that at this stage becoming sexual too soon did not allow for them to feel their emotional connection solely. Plus, being sexual too soon could elicit Yvonne's SAS. I explained to Derek that these early exercises were to build trust toward being able to be sexual.

Love Spot Variation

Another way of experiencing the Love Spot is in the following giving and receiving exercise.

Goal: To give and receive love through touch.
Preparation: Have your partner lie down on something comfortable either on his or her back or stomach. The side that is facing up should be the side that is more sensitive to receiving touch and love. You then sit next to your partner sideways, facing toward his or her head.

Directions: Put your hand on the Love Spot, that is, in the middle of his or her chest or back. Have your partner guide your hand to the right spot where he or she feels your hand with more sensation. For some people, this spot is in a quite specific place. Then each of you be quiet within yourselves as you, the giver, focuses on sending your love through your hand into your partner's body. Stay with this for five to ten minutes. Your partner focuses on receiving the love and energy that you are giving. When done, take a few minutes to share what this was like and then reverse positions. Feel the sweetness of this moment.

Receiving Touch

Goal: To enjoy the experience and connection of giving and receiving touch together.

Preparation: Decide where you want to be and what positions you each want to assume for this exercise. For example, the receiver could be lying down on the bed or on a matt or sitting in a chair. The giver can be sitting or standing.

Directions: Look back at the Receiving Touch exercise in chapter 11. Now with your partner try each of the four different types of touch: caressing, kneading, scratching, and finger touching. Start with you giving and your partner receiving. Begin with the four types of touch on your partner's arm. Then decide where else to experiment with the four types of touching. After each round of touching, talk about which type of touch your partner liked the most and why. Feel the special giving and receiving you are experiencing. Now reverse roles.

Variations of Receiving Touch: There are many ways to play with touching each other. Here are a couple:

1. With your partner lying on his or her front, draw figure eights on his or her back from the shoulders to the waist. Then, if it doesn't trigger the Alarm, make the eights from the shoulders to the top of the legs crossing at the waist.
2. With your partner again lying on his or her front and you kneeling next to him or her, put your hands at his or her waist parallel to the floor. Then extend your arms out the length of his or her body with each arm going in the opposite direction. This gives a nice stretch to your partner.

In her book *The Sexual Healing Journey* Wendy Maltz (1991) describes a number of "relearning touch" (pp. 249–285) exercises for couples in which one or both of the partners have experienced sexual trauma. Her exercises can be helpful for all women because of the effects of the SAS. She presents such touch exercises as drawing letters on each other's back with your fingers and "safe embrace" (p. 267) in which you rest your head on your partner's chest and listen to his or her heartbeat. I recommend getting her book and trying some of the exercises.

Tingling/Electric Sensations

Goal: To evoke and play with tingling/electric sensations together.

Preparation: Talk with each other about any places on your body where you can experience tingling and/or electric sensations when you touch yourself or when touched by each other. Examples might be on your neck, your inner upper arms, or your inner thighs. Also, you may have specific spots that when pressed give these sensations. For example, some people have spots in their buttocks that generate strong pleasure and releasing sensations. Once you have identified any potentially sensitive areas, talk about what type of stimulation might produce some tingling and/or electric sensations that could be enjoyable. Review the Tingling exercise in chapter 11.

Directions: Try different areas on your body to find these spots and play with eliciting sensations. Give each other directions about how to stimulate these spots. Absorb the energy generated from the tingling or slight jolt of the electric sensations.

ALLOWING

Couples Allowing exercises provide the experience of expanding the partners' sensations together. The contact allows each partner to feel more deeply and intensely. The exercises bring new sensations plus attention to experiences that are often missed because they are part of times when there is a lot of interaction happening. Following are a number of Allowing exercises for you to offer to your couple.

Spreading

Goal: To feel your partner spreading energy through your body.

Preparation: This is a continuation of the Love Spot exercise. After you have finished the Love Spot exercise and each of you are feeling more open, take turns spreading the energy as follows. Start with you giving and your partner receiving. Have your partner sit with his or her eyes closed.

Directions: After doing the Love Spot exercise, with your hands gently spread the awakened energy from your partner's chest down into his/her belly. Glide your hands from his/her chest over the stomach onto the belly with a kind of patting motion like you would do in patting a cat. Then spread the energy down your partner's arms. Talk to each other in order to know what each is experiencing and what else your partner needs to feel the spreading. Feel the movement of energy.

Expanding

Goal: Look back at the third Expanding exercise in chapter 11. In this exercise you rolled up into a ball and gradually expanded your body out of the ball. Using this same concept as a couple, you are now going to expand each other. This exercise can give each partner a wonderful feeling of being cared for.
Preparation: Begin by rolling yourself up into a ball in the middle of the bed or on a carpeted floor or mat.
Directions: Then have your partner gradually expand your body by opening you up part by part. He or she begins slowly lifting up your head, then opening your arms, then opening your legs until your body is fully open and lying down. Then your partner goes to one arm, picks up your hand and gently pulls on it expanding your arm outward. He or she does this for each limb so that you feel gently and lovingly stretched out. After you have absorbed this expanding, you change positions and you become the expander.

Sliding and Gliding

Goal: To feel each other's bodies moving sensually around on each other.
Preparation: Your partner lies on the bed. You kneel beside him or her.
Directions: Play with gliding over your reclining partner with clothes on or off. You start by lying on top of your reclining partner supporting your weight with your arms if necessary. Then you gently slide on your partner's body going to one side and then the other, moving up and down using your arms to help the movement. You can also slide by kneeling sideways over your partner's body with your knees on one side and your arms on the other. Lower your chest and slide up and down your partner's body. These movements may be awkward at first and require some practice. Feel the contact and connection of the movement.

Margo Anand (1989) describes a similar couples exercise that she calls "Slipping and Sliding." Using oils over their bodies, she suggests to partners, "Stand together, then slide your body around your partner's with the slow, undulating movements of a snake" (p. 144). Then she suggests that with one partner lying face down, the other slides sensuously over the other supporting his or her weight with arms and legs.

Rolling

Goal: How do you roll together? Gently and softly. The purpose is to move together in a complementary and connected way.

Preparation: Lie on top of your partner on the bed.

Directions: Breathe together and relax into each other. Begin in slow motion to roll off your partner onto your back while your partner also very slowly rolls up onto you. Feel the motion of each other as you move. If your bed is large enough, try another similar roll, or if not, roll back to where you started. This may be awkward at first until you get used to moving together. You may know this movement from being sexual together. When you are comfortable with rolling slowly, increase the speed. Play with different ways of moving. You could also try the following: as the person on top is rolling onto the bottom, that person could pull the partner up on top of her. Allow yourselves to have some fun with the Rolling.

Ira and Ilana liked doing the Breath of Fire together. Afterward they felt energized and were unsure what to do with this energy. When I suggested Rolling, they were excited about trying it. Both were highly energetic people and remembered rolling down hills as kids. We went through the directions and they were enthusiastic about rolling around on their bed. Both reported that the exercise was a flop the first time around because they were too rambunctious and nearly hurt each other. Each got annoyed that the other was too rough. We talked about them slowing down and rolling slowly and gently. When they tried this, they enjoyed it even though the slow pace was not easy for either of them. Through repeating this exercise, they learned about watching out for each other and integrating their movements into a flow.

Rocking

Goal: To feel the rhythm and joining together of coordinated Rocking movement.

Preparation: Lie together in a spoon position, that is, one of you lying with your backside up against the other's front, curled in together like spoons.

Directions: First snuggle together and feel the warmth of each other's bodies. When ready, start gently rocking your bodies back and forth in synch together. You do this by each pushing your chest and pelvis forward and back. Take the time you need to find a comfortable rocking rhythm. Feel the joining of your bodies in this movement. For fun you could add another option to this exercise. For this part it would be better, if your partner is a man, for you to be behind him. Imagine that you are a train slowing getting started. Your rocking motions gradually start as the train begins to move. Slowly gather speed chugging together, laughing at the silliness of this and adding some train noises together.

Scarves Exercise

Goal: Direct the couple to revisit the Scarves exercise in the Allowing exercises in chapter 12. The goal is to work with the scarves to experience the coordination and interconnection of movement.

1. Preparation: Each of you has a scarf in each of your hands.
Directions: First play with the scarves by yourselves as described in the scarves exercise in chapter 12. Then begin interweaving your scarves as you stand facing each other. Also try mirroring each other's scarf movements. For example, one partner can turn both scarves to the left while the other partner turns them to the right. Let the scarves move and flow together. Feel the energy you are creating.
2. Preparation: Have your partner stand still in a comfortable nonrestricted space.
Directions: Whirl your scarves around your partner's body. You can either walk around your partner or stand on something solid and whirl the scarves around him or her. For your partner to receive the scarves' movement, he or she can move slightly with the flow of the scarves. Feel the dance you are developing together.

Licking

Goal: To experience fun and sensual pleasure together.
Preparation: Think of something you enjoy eating that can be spread on the body, such as cheese cake or guacamole. Have the food available on a table. Sit on a bed together.
Directions: Start by putting some of the food on your partner's arm, a neutral place. Slowly lick off some of the food, taking the time to feel your partner's skin against your tongue. For the person who is being licked, let yourself feel the touch of your partner's tongue on your skin. Together

vary the types and style of licking. Take turns in each role. Then try putting some of the food on your partner's belly if you both feel ready to try a more intimate version of the exercise.

SURRENDERING

Surrendering exercises as a couple are a chance to move beyond ordinary experience into a new fullness. They are a time for partners to let go into each other and feel something greater than the two of them. As a couple the partners have a chance to transcend ordinary life and melt into each other, deeply connecting their inner spirits with one another. This may be challenging because it requires openness and trust. The following exercises are meant to help lead the partners together toward new sensations.

In Surrendering to her partner, a woman is fully giving to him or her. This requires knowing what is happening and trusting herself in her partner's hands. If her SAS is active, there is no way to surrender. In fact her SAS is meant to keep her from surrendering because it is not safe. Thus, these exercises require a full sense of safety. The previous exercises help to build trust and lead up to a woman being able to surrender to her partner. This type of surrendering can be a positive and wonderful experience. Because it can also be scary, your woman client and her partner will need careful guidance from you in these exercises.

Sounds

Goal: Making sounds together combines Allowing and Surrendering. It is a time to explore, build on each other, and have fun. The main focus of sounding together is to resonate tones and build a field of sound.
Preparation: Sit together on a bed or in chairs in a relaxed and quiet environment.
Directions: Begin by doing the Simple Breathing together. As you both inhale, let out some sounds, for example, sighing or "MMM." Feel the resonating of your sounds together.

1. Toning: Find a tone and make the same tone together, in other words, be on the same note. Make the tone on a long exhale together. This can generate an incredible vibration of sound inside each of your bodies. By being on the same frequency together, you will create resonance inside one another. When one string on a violin is plucked, the same string on another nearby violin will start vibrating. In toning you are like the violin strings.

2. Next explore the sounds of birds and animals together. Try cawing, then chirping, meowing, barking. Make your sounds at times identical and at times complementary. Feel how your sounds and you expand together.

3. Move to full releasing sounds that take you into Surrendering. Make the following sounds together, allowing yourselves to have some fun and entering into the spirit of each sound: roaring like lions, church bells ringing, sirens wailing, train whistles blowing, drumming with your hands on a table, stomping together on a wood floor, clapping, and hollering. Go back to the sounds you both most enjoy and make them again, more fully letting go into them.

Shaking and Vibrating

1. Shaking separately

Goal: To let go together.
Preparation: Stand together in an unrestricted space.
Directions: Try shaking separately and at the same time. Play some music with a good beat, and side by side go through the Total Body Shaking exercise in chapter 11. When you are fully shaking and letting out sounds, open your eyes and shake together, laughing and being totally silly.

2. Vibrating parts of each other's bodies.

Goal: To feel the relaxation and enlivening of letting your body give into the movements done to you by your partner
Preparation: Have your partner lie down on the bed. Gently put your hand on a part of his or her body.
Directions: Begin a rhythmic vibrating of that part, for example, the top of the thigh or the buttocks. Try a few different parts and try different speeds and rhythms of vibrating, looking for the one that is most pleasurable for your partner. Then switch roles. Feel what it is like to be vibrated.

Gabrielle and Carlos found that they loved vibrating each other's bodies. It took Carlos a few times to relate to the Vibrating, at first thinking that it was weird. Gabrielle was able to lead the way by her clear enjoyment of Carlos putting his hand on her buttocks and vibrating her backside. The vibration allowed her to sink into her body sensations, stop her mind chatter, and lose herself in his touch. She then directed him to vibrate her legs and then her back. Seeing her pleasure, Carlos decided to try letting Gabrielle vibrate him. He slowly warmed up to it, giving into the releasing of his tension particularly in his back.

Undulating and Writhing

Goal: To share sensuous movement together in a fun way.
Preparation: Lie on the bed together in a relaxed setting.
Directions: This is one of my favorites and is often a favorite of couples in couples workshops I have run. Pretend that you are snakes together. Slowly begin to undulate separately. You may feel quite ridiculous doing this at first. Focus on the feel of the movements. It is helpful to have tried this alone first. Review the Undulating and Writhing in chapter 11. You may need to help your partner let go into the movement. Gradually begin to move over each other, snaking around the bed. Feel the points of contact as you touch parts of each other and then keep moving. Let yourself feel slithery and smooth.

In suggesting that a couple be snakes together, it is important to determine if they are ready and able to be this playful and uninhibited together. Shamus and Kira were willing, but a bit nervous about trying this exercise. They were able to play in other ways, so I thought this would be helpful for them. We talked it through, looking at whether they were ready. At home they started taking turns caressing each other in bed with just underwear on. Then Kira lay on top of Shamus, letting herself sink into him. Slowly she began sliding on his body and he began to slither around her laughing together. As they moved, they began to be snakes hissing, sticking out their tongues, and giggling. It was quite a new and liberating experience for each of them. Particularly Kira had never imagined that she could do something like this. She recounted that starting slowly plus Shamus's gentleness and lightness of spirit helped her to feel safe and open.

Thrusting

Goal: To experience aggressive play in a safe way.
Preparation: Lie together on the bed in a relaxed setting.
Directions: Some of my couples call this riding. Begin with clothes on. Play with lying on top of each other and thrusting your pelvises simultaneously back and forth in a suggestive, but not sexual way. Then have your partner lie on the bed while you sit on top of him or her as if he or she is a horse. Have your partner thrust his or her pelvis up and down as you "ride" on top. You need to feel safe enough to do this exercise as it can elicit the SAS.

Rosira decided that she was ready to try the Thrusting exercise, imagining that she was riding Roberto like a horse. With both of them clothed Roberto lay on the bed and Rosira sat on top of his pelvis. He began thrusting his pelvis up and down as she rocked with him, pushing herself with her knees and thighs. Off they went! He loved her bouncing on top of him. After several minutes she fell off of him laughing and they hugged. In the next therapy session Rosira joyfully spoke about how she had been able to feel the thrusting movements without fear. She was, however, nervous about Roberto expecting the thrusting to become sexual the next time they tried this. He admitted it was very stimulating. This is the bind for some men in doing these exercises. We reinforced the importance of going slowly. If this exercise causes men to get an erection, it may be too much for either or both partners because it makes the exercise too sexual.

Case Study: Lexi

Lexi came to therapy to work on how shut down she felt sexually. She was often unable to be very aroused or have orgasm in her relationship with Alisha. Given that the two women had enjoyed a fulfilling sexual relationship early on, Lexi was at a loss to explain what had happened to her. She described feeling confused and lost. Alisha, she said, was at times understanding and at times impatient and frustrated with her. She described Alisha's sexual style as being like a train racing through the station with no stops. She often felt like she couldn't catch her breath during their intimacy. Experiencing Alisha as overwhelming, she often felt her body shut down. In many ways she admired Alisha's high energy and, in fact, in other areas of their life she depended on this energy. Thus, she was reluctant to push too hard for them to slow down. Coming to understand the SAS helped Lexi tremendously. As I described it and how it works, she kept saying, "Yes, that's it! Yes! That's exactly what happens!" Relieved that she was not the only one who reacted to an aggressive partner by shutting down, she then protested that Alisha was a woman, so how could the SAS apply. I explained that the SAS is something all women experience regardless of sexual orientation. Women partners can trigger the Alarm because the Alarm does not discriminate. It reacts to signals of danger without noticing who the person is.

Like many women, Lexi had experienced events in her life that helped solidify the SAS. She had been followed, cat called, and rubbed against in subways. Most disturbing for her was an experience of a man aggressively cornering her in an elevator. Fortunately, she was able to escape at one of the stops. Like many women, she had discounted this experience as having any relevance to her response to her current partner. Talking it through, she came to understand that these experiences had indeed contributed to her reactivity to Alisha's intensity sexually.

We started to work with the Ingredients and the Progressive Exercises with Lexi alone. She responded particularly well to the Simple Breathing, soft body Slapping, the T'ai Chi arms, the Rocking, and the Receiving Touch exercises, all of them soft and calming exercises. Working with the exercises to increase her energy level was more of a challenge. We had to slowly work into the Surrendering exercises such as Vibrating and Undulating. The really vigorous exercises such as Total Body Shaking were too much for her. Through the softer exercises she was able to connect with her own body rhythm and movement.

Then she was ready to transition into couple work with Alisha. She knew it wasn't going to be easy. In the beginning Alisha had understood the work Lexi was doing. Yet later, as expected, she was impatient, often asking Lexi where she was in her exercises. Understanding her own SAS helped Alisha to support Lexi in her individual work. In the couples therapy, Lexi started with an exercise that she had already done and felt ready to share with Alisha. Her main concerns were that Alisha would push her too fast and that she would not hold onto the gains she had made. I assured her that we would pace the work and deal with any issues this created.

Initially in the couples session we explored how Alisha would react to a slow pace. This brought out some of Alisha's fears about her own sexuality. She had learned that moving quickly assured her of an orgasm and jumped over some of her own inhibitions. She was, in fact, open to learning some new ways of being sexually. Not that it would be easy, she insisted.

They began with an Awakening exercise, the Tapping, a variation on Slapping. This exercise was carefully chosen by them to be gentle and slightly energetic. Each enjoyed the contact and light stimulation. We processed the exercise and their interactions. Along the way we also dealt with relationship issues as they emerged. The Love Spot Variation, an Awareness Exercise, was a small breakthrough for Alisha and Lexi. Each felt deeply moved by feeling the other's love coming through the partner's arm into her body. This exercise often creates a warmth and connection for couples. As they progressed into Allowing exercises, they tried the Expanding exercise, which opened up some laughing and a sense of play together as they each became silly, gently prying each other open and then closing each other back up. Rolling was a real challenge for Lexi. At first she didn't want to try it because she was sure Alisha would be too rough and she, Lexi, would get triggered. In fact, Alisha had visions of rolling around the floor almost like wrestling. At this point more of Alisha's resentment emerged about how careful she had to be of Lexi. Lexi broke down in tears, appealing to Alisha to understand her fear and the upset of being cornered in the elevator. This brought back a forgotten experience of Alisha's when she used to wrestle with her older brother and he wouldn't let her up. Holding her down, he would pretend to try to kiss her as she flailed around. All in fun, she thought.

We discussed how this experience had contributed to her own SAS. It had also given her a determination to be as tough and strong as her brother. Her memory softened her toward Lexi and they held each other tearfully. For homework they decided to just lie together and wait on Rolling.

The lying together felt very reassuring to both women. They stayed with this for a number of weeks, returning to the Love Spot Variation and Tapping. Once they had gained some confidence in their connection they were ready to try some Surrendering exercises. We began with one that was non-threatening to both of them, making sounds together. Each liked to sing, so we began with Toning and moved to animal sounds. They had a quite uproarious night together howling, cawing, chirping, etc. This helped them to experience letting go. We had a number of discussions about trust and releasing physically. When they were ready for another exercise, we went through a number of possibilities and they decided on Vibrating. At home they each vibrated parts of each other's bodies. This began to open up some erotic energy for each of them. We kept the limits on nonsexual stimulation. This was the beginning of their reestablishing their sexual connection. They had found enough safety and accessibility through their bodies to develop the trust that they needed to move forward.

SUMMARY

Your woman client has now had a chance to bring her earlier learning into her couple relationship or an imagined relationship through many rich experiences described in this chapter. Hopefully these experiences have brought the partners closer and the woman feels far more comfortable and safe. She has been able to calm the SAS with her partner and broaden out their intimate sharing. The couple exercises have included expanded experiences from the Ingredients and the Progressive Exercises Program. Now in chapter 14 comes a critical and challenging step: adding arousal to the woman's individual and then couple work. The experiences she has had are key to making this transition be smooth and welcomed.

Chapter Fourteen

Adding Subjective Arousal

"How can my woman client move from these exercises to becoming sexual?"

"How does she add in arousal to what she is doing?"

This chapter is about the important transition steps from the Ingredients and the Progressive Exercises to sexual experience. It introduces ways for a woman to add in subjective arousal by herself and with a partner. The exercises she has already done have been designed to make this next step more comfortable, safe, and welcomed.

"Is she ready for this, can she handle it?" you may ask. Not unless she has done the preceding work in this book. This step is about expanding her sexuality, the fourth of the Four Steps of Sexual Healing. Therefore, she needs to feel safe, to be clear about her limits, and to feel in touch with her own sense of female sexuality.

Focusing on adding subjective arousal is in keeping with Rosemary Basson's model of female sexual arousal and desire in chapter 5. Breaking with the Master and Johnson/Helen Singer Kaplan model of a linear progression from desire, excitement, plateau, orgasm to resolution, Basson advocates a circular model as follows: intimacy leads to receptivity, to subjective arousal, to arousal and response desire and back to intimacy. She emphasizes that a woman's experience of subjective arousal is more important than genital arousal.

Having opened up her body to new physical and emotional experiences in a safe comfortable way through the Ingredients and the Progressive Exercises, your woman client will have experienced greater knowledge about and intimacy with herself and her inner spirit. These exercises will have given her a special feeling of closeness to her own body. This self-intimacy can now allow for her to progress to a subjective experience of arousal, that is, arousal that she experiences as arousal. Basson has shown that women can feel physical arousal without experiencing it subjectively. For this reason, I will refer to the goal of arousal as subjective arousal.

There is also the question of desire. In Basson's model, desire is not something many women experience spontaneously, certainly not the way men often do. Desire is the result of and interacts with intimacy, receptivity, appropriate sexual stimuli, and subjective arousal. Thus, desire overlaps with and results from subjective arousal. It is not something that pops up by itself as in men. Basson writes not just of desire, but of "responsive" desire because women's desire is in a wider context of stimuli. During these exercises that bring out subjective arousal, women will at times also feel desire. I do not focus on desire here because it is not the goal. Making desire the goal for women often triggers the SAS. It says, "You should be like a man." It pushes women into experiences that make them vulnerable by isolating desire from safety and intimacy. Women have learned that feeling desire is unsafe, dangerous, and attached to images of "bad" women. At times I will discuss desire as part of the interconnection with subjective arousal.

When introducing subjective arousal, it is also important for women to stay connected to their inner spirit. Often women disconnect from themselves when sexual feelings start to develop. These exercises are not isolated, "try to get turned on" exercises. They flow out of the work in the previous chapters, connecting sexual feelings not only with intimacy, but also with a deep sense of connection to the spirit both within us and beyond us.

THE STEPS

The three primary ways for your women clients to add subjective arousal to the previous exercises are as follows:

1. To integrate her genital and her breast sensations with the rest of her body.
2. To let some subjective arousal emerge naturally as she does the Ingredients and the Progressive Exercises.
3. To let subjective arousal emerge naturally with her partner doing couple exercises.

The primary goal in this transition is for your women clients to be able to add subjective arousal in by themselves so that they can claim their sexuality as their own and not be dependent on a partner. Women need to be able to feel their sexuality by themselves much as men do. If they can bring their own sense of their sexual selves to the table, they can feel less reactive, less of a victim, and much more secure. To be able to have control of their own sexual response is a powerful tool to disarm the SAS. Then women won't startle so easily, become scared, and be sent into a numb shutting down. If they are strong in their own right sexually and are able to make choices, they are less susceptible to the SAS. If they have given away their sexuality, their partners can more easily scare them, especially if their partners are aggressive sexually. When women reclaim their sexuality, they are more prepared. Like a sensei in martial arts, they are more centered and able to take on perceived aggressors without losing themselves.

For some women adding in subjective arousal without a partner may be too much of a stretch. It may go against too many negative prohibitions from growing up. These women may need to take this step *with* their partners. However, they can still take the subjective arousal experience with a partner back into themselves and own it as their own. This is, in fact, a crucial step even for women who can add in subjective arousal on their own.

The focus of this chapter is adding in subjective arousal, not self-stimulation and not having orgasm. Self-stimulation and orgasms are important topics in dealing with women's sexuality, but topics that are beyond the scope of this book. This book is about opening up women's body sensations including subjective arousal. I recommend Lonnie Barbach's (2000) book *For Yourself* for working with self-stimulation to get to orgasm. The information in her book can be very helpful for working with the exercises here, but the goal is different.

As you guide your woman client through these exercises, remember to help her choose exercises that appeal to her, that are appropriate for where she is in this work, and that she can physically do without discomfort. These exercises, as all the exercises, are done by the woman in the privacy of her home.

ON HER OWN

Integrating Sexual Body Parts with the Rest of the Body

An important step in being able to add in subjective arousal is for a woman to integrate her breasts and her genitals with the rest of her body. For many women their genitals don't exist or worse. Vulvas are associated with menstruation, urination, yeast infections, and/or violation. Breasts are associated with male needs and external attention and approval. For women to be comfortable in their bodies, they need to make their breasts and genitals their own. These directions are written for therapists to give to their women clients.

1. Begin by getting to know your genitals and breasts. Many women don't know their vulva and have never seen it.

    a. Finding your vulva and breasts: Start by looking at a diagram of your vulva so you know your geography. Using your forefinger, touch your vulva area finding your clitoris, your labia, the entrance to your vagina, and your perineum. It is helpful to explore your genitals with touch to get to know yourself in a perhaps less threatening way before the next step of looking at your genitals. Also explore your breasts making circular movements around your breasts to feel the shape of them. Some women have sexually sensitive nipples and some don't. Their nipples may be part of their SAS, which can keep them from being responsive. Breasts, as we know, are such a focal point for men that they tend to grab them and over-stimulate the nipples, causing women to pull away. To integrate your nipples with your breasts, pass over them gently returning to the circular movement around your breasts.

    b. Looking at your genitals: This can be a challenge for women, many of whom have never seen their genitals. They are that thing that is "down there." They are smelly and dirty. Imagine this: they are quite amazing and beautiful. To set a framework for appreciating your genitals, start by looking at some of Georgia O'Keefe's flowers. You can see some online at http://www.google.com. (Type in Georgia O'Keefe and click on Images for Georgia O'Keefe.) In her flowers are the beauty of women's vulvas. Imagine your vulva as wonderful and special like her flowers. Then I suggest you look at drawings or pictures of other women's vaginas before looking at your own. This will give you a context for seeing yourself and show you the amazing variety of shapes and configurations of vulvas. You can see drawings in *Sex for One: The Joy of Selfloving* by Betty Dodson (1996). Now get a mirror and take a peek at your own vulva. I say a peek, because this may be difficult or embarrassing for you. This may be a "No-no" from way back. It is best to do this when you are not menstruating. You may be surprised, unimpressed, "grossed out," or intrigued. Let yourself think, "Imagine that. All these years and I have looked rarely or not at all at such an important part of my body." Then let yourself look longer. Find your clitoris, your inner labia and outer labia, the entrance to your vagina, and your perineum.

2. Now start to connect your genitals with your whole body. It is very important to keep your genitals integrated with the rest of your body. Oversexualization of women has detached our genitals and breasts

from the rest of us. Spreading from chapter 11 is a very helpful way to interconnect parts of the body. Below is an adaptation of the Spreading exercise for this chapter.

Spreading

Spreading involves taking a sensation in your body and moving it to another part of your body with your hands. When the sensation spreads, it grows, it includes more of your body, and you feel more full. When you discover that you can actually make sensations move into more of your body, you can feel amazed and empowered.

Goals: 1) To move warmth from your chest down into your belly, and 2) to learn how to spread energy through your lower body to your vulva and back up to your breasts and upper body.

Preparation: Sit in a comfortable chair or lie on your bed in a relaxing setting.

Directions: Start with some Simple Breathing to create energy in your chest. Then place your palms on your chest. Begin to spread the energy in your chest by slowly moving your hands straight down over your diaphragm to your belly, down over your pubic mound, over your vulva, and back to your belly. Then bring your palms around to the side of your pelvis and back up the sides of your chest, over your breasts, up to your neck and face, and back to the center of your chest. Feel the energy move through your body and feel the interconnection of your body areas. Breathe fully. The purpose of this touch is exploratory. It is not yet for subjective arousal. Feel the connection of your vulva to your breasts and the rest of your body.

Letting Subjective Arousal Emerge

In the beginning of doing the Ingredients and Progressive Exercises, the point is to NOT focus on subjective arousal. Your woman client is experimenting with 1) experiencing and expanding her body sensations in new and fuller ways, and 2) experiencing the elements of the sexual experience without the subjective arousal in order to not trigger the SAS. Subjective arousal may 1) take over the experience, 2) trigger the SAS, 3) be too distracting, and 4) interfere with the experiences she is learning to feel.

As your client has practiced the exercises, she has begun to open physically, emotionally, and spiritually. At first this may be unnerving, scary, and exciting all at the same time. The more exercises she has done and the more she has repeated the exercises, the more she has become comfortable with her experiences. Many wonderful things are happening. Whole new dimensions of feeling are developing in her body. For example, she may have come to know and appreciate the sensations of Rocking, Vibrating, Surrendering, laughing, chirping, breathing, Thrusting, etc. As she is comfortable with these experiences, sensual and sexual feelings may start to develop on their own.

In the beginning the goal was to not get sexually aroused. However, once she has expanded her experiences and feels her body in new ways, she is likely to be ready to begin to allow for the possibility of sexual feelings of subjective arousal. With this may come feelings of desire. For some women this won't happen and they will need to be more focused on direct stimulation to feel subjectively aroused. For others the sensations will happen on their own through the breathing and the movements. If they do happen on their own, at this point in the woman's work guide her to let them be there and to imagine that they are spreading through her body. An important goal when adding subjective arousal is to broaden arousal beyond just genital experience. Genital sensations can be very limited, intense, and disconnected from the rest of a woman's body. In our culture sex is all about the genitals, usually the penis. So women have come to think that for them it must also be about their genitals, with the addition of their breasts because they are so fascinating to men. This restrictive view is part of what is inhibiting.

Guide your woman client to start to be conscious and to direct her attention to adding subjective arousal. Certain exercises are particularly conducive for this, for example the Genital Breathing and the Pelvic Rock Breathing. It is worth repeating the directions for these exercises here to help you guide your woman client to take these breathing exercises to another level. I add to the previous directions for these exercises a focusing on subjective arousal.

1. Genital Breathing

Goal: To connect your breathing to your genitals in order to open yourself to the experience of subjective arousal.

Preparation: Sit upright in a comfortable chair or lie on a mat or carpet on the floor in a relaxing environment.

Directions: Now add your genitals to the above breathing (who thinks about their genitals when breathing?). Imagine your vagina and vulva to be like a mouth (we even have lips there). As you inhale, imagine drawing air into your vagina and letting it expand and relax. As you exhale, imagine that you are pushing the air out through your vagina. Be aware of the sensations in your genitals and pelvis as you do this. The first few times you do this to add subjective arousal, it may feel awkward. You may feel nothing. Keep doing the exercise as these sensations take time to experience.

Encourage your woman client to add to this exercise the possibility of experiencing some subjective arousal. She may feel a warm tingling sensation in her genitals as she breathes. Encourage her to welcome in sensual awakening sensations in her genitals. She may also feel sensations of desire. Encourage her to include her genitals rather than exclude them. Because it is automatic to exclude them, women don't realize that not feeling sexual feelings during experiences such as these takes training. And trained they are since a young age! When a part of one's body is not mentioned, then the experiences associated with it are taboo and pushed out of awareness so that they then don't exist. Thus, we are working at reversing many years of experience.

2. Pelvic Rock Breathing

This is a potentially powerful breathing and rocking exercise. It takes some coordination and practice before it flows smoothly.

Goal: To open up your pelvis to increased sensation and to connect pelvic movements to your breathing in order to open yourself to the experience of subjective arousal.

Preparation: Lie on a carpet or mat the floor on your back with your knees up and your feet on the floor in a comfortable environment.

Directions:

Step 1: Do the above Genital Breathing.

Step 2: Now focus just on moving your pelvis in the following way:

Arch your back up at the waist rocking your genitals toward the floor. Then reverse the movement flattening your back down and slightly raising your lower buttocks off the floor.

Step 3: Now combine steps 1 and 2 so that as you arch your back up and rock your genitals toward the floor, you relax and open your vagina imagining that you inhale through it. Imagine that you are making a space for the air to enter your pelvis. Then exhale as you flatten your back and pull your lower buttocks up very slightly, imagining that you can exhale through your vagina.

Think: arch, open and inhale, then flatten, contract and exhale. Feel the sensations in your genitals as you breathe and rock.

This exercise works directly with the genitals, breathing through them and contracting and releasing them. These movements may well stimulate sensations of warmth and subjective arousal. Tell your client to let these sensations grow and develop as she breathes and moves. She may feel warmth, tingling, and/or waves of sensation.

Certain Ingredients movement experiences are readily associated with sexual movements such as Undulating, Licking, and Thrashing. To include subjective arousal into these exercises, direct your woman client to first imagine the possibility of arousal accompanying what she is doing and then to let positive sexual associations come into her mind such as an enjoyable sexual time. Or she can fantasize a possible loving and sexual scene in which she is making these movements. The goal is to let the subjective arousal happen, to invite it in and not force it. With the subjective arousal may come feelings of desire. Advise your client to feel the sense of wanting that may be developing. An example of using an Ingredient exercise is Vibrating. You can direct your woman client as follows. Begin with using your hand to vibrate your thighs as described in the Vibrating exercise in chapter 11. Feel the sensation of the vibration as it spreads through your upper legs. Come close to your vulva, vibrating your upper inner thighs on both legs. Then move one of your hands on top of your pubic mound and vulva and continue vibrating, letting the sensations spread into your genitals. Do this for a few seconds and go back to your thighs. Spread the vibrations by moving your hands to other areas such as your buttocks and back, connecting all the areas. Treat this as an exploration to experience whatever sensations you have rather than expecting that you will experience subjective arousal right away.

You can also help your woman client to combine exercises to enhance the possibility of arousal feelings, for example, Simple Breathing with Thrusting, or Shaking with Rocking. Other exercises that you can suggest to her for allowing subjective arousal to develop are the Butterfly and the acupressure points in chapter 12.

Another way for a woman to add subjective arousal is to combine sensual music with any of the exercises. Sensual music is subjective for each person, yet there are certain types of music that many people experience as sensual. These include such music as Middle Eastern music, R&B, slow winding jazz, and South American flute music. Ask your client which type of music is sensual for her. Find out if she has any recordings of this type of music and if not, help her find out how she can get a recording (such as on iTunes or Amazon.com). When she has a recording, tell her to put on the music while she is doing these exercises. At first tell her to let the music enter her body and let it resonate inside her. Once she feels the sensuality of the music in her body, encourage her to let the music flow through her, bringing her whole body alive. The music itself can bring out feelings of subjective arousal.

WITH HER PARTNER

In the partner exercises your woman client can introduce subjective arousal in the same ways as above either by 1) being conscious of subjective arousal that may develop in the exercises, or 2) doing particular movements that she associates with arousal.

Before your woman client begins any of these exercises with her partner, advise her to be sure to do quite a few of the couples exercises to connect together physically in a safe way that explores opening up her body and that does not set off her SAS. It is important that she and her partner have been doing these exercises over time and then again right before they begin this new journey together. This brings in the very important factor of intimacy, which Basson writes is critical for the development of subjective arousal and responsive desire. Direct your client to begin with couple exercises such as the Simple Breathing, the Love Spot, Spreading, and/or Rolling from chapter 11.

When your client is ready, encourage her to let subjective arousal emerge during couple exercises. It is helpful at first for her to not talk about her it, but to let it be her own experience. Telling her partner adds another layer of complexity such as self-consciousness and partner expectations. If her partner asks her what she is experiencing, she can just say, "I'm enjoying my body sensations."

Advise your client to let herself just enjoy any subjective arousal that occurs and to not do anything in particular with the sensations. Letting subjective arousal emerge with a partner can happen in much the same way as by herself as described above. As your client gains more experience and confidence in her ability to let the sexual feelings happen, sharing her experiences with her partner becomes more natural and easy.

Suggest to your client that she pick exercises that she has already done alone to let subjective arousal emerge, such as Genital Breathing or Shaking. She needs to decide what she would like her partner to be doing during this experience. Having her partner hold her lovingly is often the most helpful. If she is moving around, she may want her partner to move in the same way with her.

From chapter 13 also help your client pick couples exercises that are conducive to letting subjective arousal emerge. Tell her to first look back to those couples exercises that she chose and reread the directions. Then consider together how she could add in letting subjective arousal emerge. Here are some examples to describe to her.

1. Tingling: When doing this exercise, pick spots on your body that could possibly tingle or feel electric in a sensual way, leading to subjective arousal. There may be such spots in your buttocks and/or the soles of your feet. Have your partner gently press on these spots. Feel the possible sparkle of sexual energy.

2. Spreading: After your partner spreads your energy from your chest down over your belly, have him or her spread it to your pelvis and pubic area. This does not include direct stimulation of your vulva at this point. Feel the energy as it flows into this area.

3. Rocking: In the couples Rocking exercise you are spooning together and rocking back and forth. Let the rocking motion come into your pelvis and vulva, possibly carrying you away into subjective arousal sensations.

4. Licking: This is a very sensual movement. When you are ready, pick parts of your body that could response sensually to being licked, for example your neck or your inner thighs. Open yourself for delicious subjective arousal and desire feelings.

5. Undulating: This is a wonderful couple exercise with the possibility of feeling quite sensual. As you make the motions of being snakes together, let yourself feel the sensuous energy entering your vulva and opening up possible subjective arousal and desire.

6. Thrusting: Once you have gained a sense of safety with the thrusting motions, let yourself be open to subjective arousal and desire being part of the experience. To do this, you need to feel in charge and not overwhelmed by your partner's responses. You need to be ready to embrace aggressive movements being exciting.

The focus so far has been on your woman client letting herself feel subjective arousal with her partner. What about the partner's arousal? These exercises are likely to be stimulating to the partner. A male partner may well get an erection. It is important to discuss this with your client. Both she and her male partner need to understand that an erection means enjoyment and is not a sexual demand. This may be difficult for either one or both to accept. It is a crucial part of this work. Learning how to experience subjective arousal without having to do anything is vital to this work having its intended effect of opening up the woman's sexuality. We can enjoy sexual feelings without having to take action on our sensations. Explain this concept to your woman client so that she can understand this and can convey this concept to her partner. Help her to reassure her partner, male or female, that this step is vital for both of them. The partner too can learn how to savor arousal feelings rather than rush through them. This process will eventually lead to sexual activity, but not now. Feeling sexual feelings without having to take action is very reassuring for a woman because it gives her the space to have her sexual feelings and not shut down, that is, not have the Sexual Alarm System go into effect. Holding subjective arousal feelings, embracing them, and flowing with them is a wonderful experience.

Rita and Cort had greatly enjoyed the Vibrating exercise. Before getting to this exercise, they had done the Simple Breathing, the Receiving Touch, and the Spreading exercises. They had worked through some of the blocks that had arisen and felt ready to add subjective arousal to their experience. In fact, during the Vibrating exercise, both had felt some spontaneous tingling and warmth in their genitals. They decided to expand their Vibrating, making it more vigorous and briefly including sexual parts of their bodies. Both found this quite arousing. I cautioned them to not move too quickly. We discussed how to experience and enjoy these feelings of sexual arousal without having to act on them. Cort was annoyed and unsure that he wanted to hold back on sexual actions. When he came to understand the importance for Rita of not acting, he was able to modulate his arousal. This brought them closer, allowing Rita to feel safe in experiencing her subjective arousal without pressure to act. I reassured them that the goal was to get to sexual interactions.

SUMMARY

Adding subjective arousal into your woman client's experiences involves several steps: connecting her sexual parts with the rest of her body, letting subjective arousal emerge by herself, and letting subjective arousal emerge with her partner. This chapter gives numerous exercises for these steps. This part of a woman's growth is tender and exciting. Through the suggestions in this chapter your client is on the road to owning her own sexuality as a woman. There may still be some blocks she will encounter. If these blocks are deep seated, she may need to do further internal work directly confronting the SAS in ways described in chapter 15.

Chapter Fifteen

Working Through the Sexual Alarm System

What if a woman has significant emotional blocks that get in the way of moving beyond the SAS? In addition to the exercises presented in this book she may need to directly confront underlying issues and emotions that contribute to creating the SAS. Furthermore, there may be some behaviors that trigger that Sexual Alarm System that a woman feels are too important to put aside, for example, kissing and orgasm. So, how can a woman learn to decode the Sexual Alarm System? Working through the SAS is part of this work and involves a number of possible approaches. Here are several possible routes.

TELLING THE STORIES

Women need to tell their SAS-related stories—stories of scary events that happened to them, stories of events that almost happened to them, stories of events that happened to women close to them, and even stories of events that they read about. Telling the stories accomplishes a number of things: provides emotional release, helps women to not feel so alone, helps women recognize the real impact of these events on their sexuality, normalizes their fear and their SAS, builds bonds to other women, and helps women learn how to manage in the world. Many of women's stories are hidden or denied. They feel shameful or seem so ordinary as to not be worth mentioning. Telling the stories brings them out of hiding.

The stories vary all over the map. They may be about the boyfriend who insisted on having sex three times a day, or the man who made sexual comments at work, or the time the older man lurked around the playground offering quarters to girls to ride on his bicycle with him. Once a group of women get going, they all have stories to tell. In therapy women all have stories to tell even when they think they don't. One of my clients needs to tell me each time a new male public figure is caught cheating on his wife because her ex-husband cheated on her. She often has a new story. Telling is part of her therapy.

RELEASING EMOTIONS RELATED TO THE TRIGGERS

Women can work with triggering behaviors by allowing their emotions to emerge. As their emotions come out, they then may need to cry, tremble, and/or act out anger (yell, pound the bed, etc.) If women do this with their partners, their partners need to be able to handle the women's emotions and provide healing support. Women need to be able to trust their partners with their feelings. If they do this alone, they need to be able to let out their feelings and to be able the handle the impact. Often it is helpful for a woman to have therapeutic help in order to work with releasing her feelings. The therapist can guide a woman to gradually release her emotions in an appropriate way, making sure that she feels safe and grounded. This technique is not recommended for Alarm reactions related to sexual trauma unless the woman has done trauma therapy work.

COGNITIVE BEHAVIORAL ANXIETY MANAGEMENT

An effective cognitive behavioral technique for dealing with anxiety involves working with the thoughts that incite anxiety. A woman learns to recognize the thoughts that elicit anxiety and she evaluates the evidence for and against her concerns. She looks at the odds of the peril existing in her real life, viewing her predictions of danger as ideas rather than truths. This shows her how often her anxieties are false alarms. With the SAS there are many false alarms. A key concept in working with anxiety is identifying your "security moves." These are described in Babior and Goldman's (1996) book *Panic, Anxiety & Phobias* as "a variety of strategies in order to avert disaster" (p. 75). They include avoidance, distractions, and hyper focusing. Babior and Goldman write that one, "kind of security move involves trying to escape from your physical sensations by distracting yourself" (p. 76).

Babior and Goldman (1996) recommend the following cognitive steps for working through a feared situation: 1) expose yourself in your imagination to a low-level anxiety situation, 2) begin slow gentle breathing and relaxing, and 3) reassure the frightened part of you with the rational part of you by using the evidence against the feared danger being true. These steps are the opposite of security moves, which take you away from the feared situation. For a more detailed description of their approach, I highly recommend reading their book.

How would a woman use this approach with the SAS, especially since the fears underlying the SAS are quite real and are reinforced daily in the media and real life experiences? The key is recognizing that the fears triggered in an intimate relationship are not usually based on the reality of that relationship, with the exception, of course, of abusive relationships and highly insensitive partners. It is important for a woman to assess whether or not she really is in danger. If she is, she needs her SAS and she needs to stop the situation. If she assesses that she is not in danger, then she can use this cognitive behavioral technique to help her diminish her SAS. So, for example, if the fear that is elicited when her trusted partner pats her on the rear end is that she is about to be sexually violated, her fear is not reality. If when she and her trusted partner are kissing and hugging and her partner reaches for her genitals, she freezes because she fears being forced to be sexual, her fear does not match the situation. As a woman learns to separate her fears from what is true, she may need her partner to help her with reassurances and caring. As a therapist, you may want to teach these cognitive behavioral techniques to your women clients to help them deal with their SASs.

Desensitization

Desensitization is another cognitive behavioral technique that involves a woman first clearly identifying triggers that set off her SAS. She establishes a hierarchy of situations from the least triggering to the most triggering. Then she begins visualizing her least triggering situation and coupling it with relaxation techniques. She moves up the hierarchy step by step, coupling each situation with the relaxation. Along the way when anxiety kicks in, she stops to relax before progressing and/or goes back to a previous step and repeats it. This work is first done by the woman herself. She may then incorporate this technique into the work with her partner with you, the therapist, as the guide. For example, Margie, whose father gave her wet kisses, couldn't stand mouth kisses with any wetness. She and her partner began with dry kisses on her arm. These were non-threatening and pleasurable. Then they progressed through a number of steps until she could accept dry kisses on her check. At each step Margie used relaxation techniques to help with her anxiety. Slowly she learned to feel pleasure with each step so that she could begin to be kissed on the mouth with some wetness. Often this work needs to be done with a trained behavioral therapist. For further various cognitive behavioral approaches, the reader is referred to D. H. Barlow and M. G. Craske (2007), and J. Rygh and W. C. Sanderson (2004).

OTHER THERAPIES

There are other forms of therapy that work on a subtle mind/body level for helping people work through the effects of fear, anxiety and the fight flight response. These approaches can be used to deal with the SAS. Hypnotherapy is one approach. Others are described below.

Self Regulation Therapy

Self Regulation Therapy is described as follows by the Canadian Foundation for Trauma Research and Education:

> Self Regulation Therapy (SRT) is a non-cathartic mind/body approach aimed at diminishing excess activation in the nervous system. It has its basis in neurobiology and reflects our innate capacity to flexibly respond to novelty or threat. Significant overwhelming events at anytime in one's life can result in changes in the nervous system that negatively impact the way a person feels and relates to others. SRT enables the nervous system to integrate overwhelming events and brings balance to the nervous system. SRT works by providing a safe, contained environment in which the individual can complete the thwarted responses of fight, flight or freeze. By resourcing the client, new neural pathways are developed to flexibly manage daily challenges or stressors. Once the nervous system is balanced, individuals are able to experience joy, closeness in relationships, and vitality and resilience in the body. (*Canadian Foundation for Trauma Research and Education,* 2011)

Visualizations and Mantras

Imagery and verbal phrases are yet other ways to help a woman develop a positive sense of herself as a sexual being. These techniques are widely used to counter tension and anxiety. In dealing with the SAS, you can use the techniques with your woman client to help her build a positive counterforce within to help diminish and/or override the SAS. Developing a positive visualization first involves your client finding a place to sit comfortably and relax. Then she visualizes a safe place, either a real place or imagined place. As she sees this place, then she pictures herself there enjoying and taking in the atmosphere. Any number of positive images may be used, for example, seeing herself wearing beautiful clothing that makes her feel sensual and radiant. She needs to allow herself the time to absorb these sensations. If she is ready, she can visualize images that are more sexual, always focusing on what feels good and what enhances a positive sense of herself. As an example, a woman can visualize herself receiving safe kisses that make her feel loved and cared for.

A mantra is a positive phrase about you that you repeat to yourself silently. Have your woman client first write down all the positive phrases she feels or would like to feel about herself as a sensual sexual being and about sexuality in general. Then she goes through the list looking for a phrase that is somewhat true and is just a bit of a stretch beyond where she is, but still imaginable. If it is too far beyond reality, she will not connect with it and it will make her feel worse. The phrase also needs to resonate inside of her and evoke an uplifting feeling. Once she finds a phrase, she says it over and over inside, letting it settle into her and adapting the words until it is right. She then repeats the mantra to herself regularly to help her feel good about herself. Examples include, "I am a warm and sensual woman," "Being sexual is natural and loving." One of my favorites came from a woman in a workshop who disliked her body because she thought it was too hairy. She announced her new mantra had become "My body is like a warm tropical rain forest." Heiman and LoPiccolo (1988) describe developing, "self-efficacy" (p. 61) statements that are similar to mantras. "These are sentences that stress the strengths and resources you have in overcoming negative emotions" (p. 61). They are part of cognitive restructuring techniques that they advocate.

Positive Models

I encourage women to think of someone they know or know of who embodies a positive sense of sexuality and personal power. Women need models of other women that they can emulate and internalize. They can take the energy and strength of these models into themselves saying, "If she can be like that, then I can too." When I ask women to think of such models, they struggle to come up with people. Many initially think of sexy women who do not have a positive sense of sexuality and personal power, for example Pamela Anderson and Brittney Spears. Secondly, they think of women who have a sense of confidence and power, but not sexuality, for example, Hillary Clinton. But who combines these qualities? Who seems comfortable in her body and conveys both sensuality and strength? A few women can think of a friend or acquaintance. The names of public figures who come up frequently are Queen Latifah and Susan Sarandon. When a woman can find a role model, I encourage her to imagine what it is like to be inside that woman's body and to be out in the world. I ask her what she imagines experiencing. If she can feel the combination of sexuality and personal power, I then guide her to breathe in those qualities and sense what it would be like to feel those in herself.

Model Mugging and Self-defense

Many women were not brought up to feel strong in their bodies. Sports were for tomboys. Being feminine meant being delicate. Title Nine, making sports equally accessible to boys and girls, has changed this in many ways. Young girls now can come to feel energy and strength in their bodies through such sports as soccer, track, and basketball. Does this translate into a sense of power in dealing with assault? If so, it is still not enough. There is still a strong physical power differential between men and women, resulting in intimidation. Women need to specifically learn how to deal with an attack that could happen or has happened. Self-defense courses teach women specific skills for self-protection. Women are taught strategic skills such as kicking a man's groin, poking his eyes, stepping on his feet. They are also taught psychological strategies such as how to recognize potentially dangerous situations and how to deal with a man who is threatening. A helpful website is the Women's Self-defense Institute at http://www.self-defense-mind-body-spirit.com.

Model Mugging is an intense program that has helped many women gain the skills and psychological strength to face attackers. Women are not only taught self-defense skills, but they get to practice them on a male padded model who acts out scenes of attack. After initially practicing techniques, women develop individual scenes to act out such as a man coming into a simulated bedroom. The woman knows ahead of time what she is going to do and is coached along the way. The padded attacker then acts out his part. The other women in the group cheer each woman along, giving her more courage to face her attacker. One woman who went through this intensive training told me after that she was no longer afraid. The Model Mugging motto is "Be the Victor, and not a Victim." Below is a description from their website of their program:

- Female and male instructor teams work in a supportive environment
- Learn through realistic scenario-based training
- Practice full-force physical techniques against a padded assailant
- Understand the dynamics of sex crimes and sex offender typologies
- Develop the mindset to use skills effectively
- Use the power of voice and body language for boundary setting and de-escalation strategies
- Learn to use fear and experience the power of your body
- Course structure is sensitive to trauma survivors
- Small group classes provide personalized instruction

(*Model Mugging*, 2010)

SUMMARY

There are many ways for women to work through the deeper emotional blocks that underlie the SAS. This chapter presents a number of these approaches, such as emotional releasing, cognitive behavioral techniques, and Model Mugging. These approaches can supplement the exercises presented in this book, especially when a woman needs a deeper level of work in her therapy.

Chapter 16 presents a summary of the book and explores ways of addressing women's sexual issues that are beyond the approach of this book. There are many programs, books, groups, etc., that deal with issues related to the SAS. This chapter samples some hopeful and helpful approaches for girls and women.

Chapter Sixteen

Summary and Other Approaches for Dealing with the Sexual Alarm System

BOOK SUMMARY

As we walk out into the parking lot, we grab our keys. We walk quickly, looking around to see what men may be around. Where are they? What do they look like? What are they doing? It's twelve o'clock at night.

The elevator arrives. It's going up. We are going to the tenth floor. Inside is a lone man. We quickly assess him and whether it is safe to be alone with him in an enclosed, locked-in space. We let the elevator doors close and wait for the next one.

Why do we do these behaviors? *Because we know that as women our sexuality puts us in danger.* We learn this at an early age being girls, watching TV, watching our mothers. Because of this danger, a protective barrier develops around us. I call this the Sexual Alarm System, or SAS. Part I of this book addresses understanding the SAS. Because sexual danger is always a possibility, all women have an SAS. It is a matter of survival. The SAS is like a house alarm. Whenever a man, or even a woman, comes toward us in a way that we experience as threatening, the Alarm goes off. Often the Alarm is triggered both without our even knowing it and when there is no real danger. There are four steps to how the Alarm works.

1. We are wired. Neurologically the SAS is ingrained from an early age. It becomes part of our fight/flight system.
2. Something happens. Something crosses the boundary and the Alarm goes off.

3. We go into high alert. We are watching, waiting, ready. We may not be aware of this hyper-alert state because it is so ingrained and automatic. We may then go into action to protect ourselves, walking more quickly, pulling away, flinching.
4. We withdraw and shut down, turning off any possibility of a sexual response. We become cooler and more constrained. The curtain drops and our bodies become heavier and tighter.

The SAS affects our lives on a daily basis. It affects where we drive, how we dress, where we walk, who we look at, etc.

Men do not have a SAS. They don't have to worry about a woman sexually assaulting them (with the exception of boys who are sexually assaulted by women). Thus, men don't understand women's behaviors and often add to the SAS.

There are several categories of behaviors that trigger the SAS.

1. Impersonal, non-mutual, forceful behaviors done to women, such as grabbing, holding down, and slapping.
2. Behaviors within a relationship that remind a woman of the above behaviors. A man may grab his partner's butt thinking this will turn her on, but it has the opposite effect.
3. Behaviors that a woman once enjoyed and now fears. As a young woman trying to prove herself sexually, a woman may have participated in sexual behaviors that now scare her.

There are also specific behavioral violations that trigger the SAS.

1. Physical violations such as touch, movement, and sounds. These include such movements as aggressive touch from a partner that signals that sex is next.
2. Images of women gyrating, appearing in sexual poses in magazines apparently luring men into sex.

Physiology plays a critical role in the SAS. The SAS becomes part of women's instinctual response to danger. Instincts are a complex interweaving of inherited and learned patterns of behavior. The SAS becomes part of the neuron-chemical alerting system that prompts the body to react to stress and danger and thus is wired into a woman's fight/flight response system. It becomes, then, part of the protective instinct necessary for survival. Thus, a woman's response to triggers of the SAS is not under her control, an important factor for women and their partners to understand. It often is a relief for women and their partners to realize that a woman pulling away from being sexual is not necessarily a personal response to her partner. It may well be that the partner is triggering the SAS.

There are a number of background factors that are important in understanding the Sexual Alarm System. Part II of this book presents the history of women's sexuality, the history of sex therapy and working with women's sexual issues, the sexual development of girls, and additional issues that contribute to women's fear of sexuality.

Throughout history women and their sexuality have not fared well. From earliest recorded history women were the property of men. Through classical times and early Christian times women were considered inferior, weak, immoral, and a threat to the integrity of men's souls. Everything from the size of a woman's brain to the temperature of her body to the existence of her uterus has been used to prove women's inferiority and sexual depravity. In modern history we have seen many advances for women in property rights, voting rights, and control over their own bodies. Are we better off? Yes, definitely and also no. Women are still objectified and victimized at an alarming rate all over the world.

The field of sex therapy has many contributors to understanding women's sexuality. One of the most significant for understanding the Sexual Alarm System is Rosemary Basson. Her model of how women function sexually stresses the importance of intimacy in providing the context for becoming sexual for women. Intimacy creates safety, meaning, and connection for women. These are crucial factors in deactivating or going around the SAS.

There are many wonderful approaches to working with women's sexual issues. Lonnie Barbach (1983) was one of the pioneers with her book *For Yourself*, which taught women about their bodies and about becoming orgasmic. Since then any number of very helpful books have been written. My book is different in its focus on the specific body responses that make up and are a necessary part of the sexual experience for women.

We have gone from desexualizing women to the oversexualization of girls and women. The sexualization of girls is frightfully prevalent today. Sexual attitudes, behaviors, and expectations are imposed on girls beyond their capacity to understand, to integrate, and to react appropriately. There are beauty pageants for toddlers and bikinis for elementary school girls. Girls and teens are expected to look sexy to be popular and to sell products such as makeup and music videos. How a girl experiences her developing sexuality is beside the point.

Other factors such as family history, medicine, and attitudes about lesbianism further contribute to women's fear of their sexuality and therefore to the development of the SAS. A woman's mother often teaches her to fear her sexuality. A father often denies his daughter's sexuality. A woman's medical experiences regarding her sexuality often contribute to her detachment from her body. Today there are efforts to change this and to better inform women through TV shows, books, and better doctoring. For a girl to discover that she is attracted to someone of her own gender is often frightening. Although there is a dramatic shift in some areas toward homosexuality, prejudices and victimization persist.

Part III of this book addresses ways of working with the Sexual Alarm System. In this section I look at addressing men directly, ways of going around and working through the SAS, exercises for helping women discover their bodies in order to be able to be sexual, working with couples, and adding subjective arousal to the sexual experience. Programs that help women address other factors that contribute to the SAS complete the book.

What to do about men and the SAS? Men don't understand the SAS because it is not part of their experience. So, in fact, they need to be addressed directly. I write chapter 9 for therapists to talk to directly to men to inform them about the SAS and to give them empathy with their dilemma in relating to women sexually. I give concrete suggestions therapists can offer men in dealing with the SAS. For example, I suggest men help their partners figure out what triggers their SAS and learn ways to help them go around the SAS.

Are there ways to go around the SAS? Yes. They involve finding ways to connect to a woman that do not trigger the Alarm. Examples include approaching a woman from the front, touching her first on the shoulder, saying her name. These actions do not trigger the SAS because they are personal and familiar. The crucial factor is that they signal safety, a prime condition for a woman to be able to be sexual. These specific actions in the context of an intimate relationship can make a huge difference in a woman feeling safe enough to access her sexual feelings.

What can a woman do herself to be more comfortable in her body and to diminish the effects of the SAS? To counter the shutting down effects of the SAS, I have developed two categories of exercises that help women open up their bodies and prepare themselves for sexual feelings.

The first set of exercises is what I call the Ingredients. I realized in my work with women that there are many ingredients to being sexual besides sexual arousal. I came to see that if a woman could develop a level of comfort with these ingredients, she could then be much more ready to welcome in sexual arousal. This comfort with the ingredients would help her know her body, help her relax into her body, and diminish the tensing effects of the SAS. I then developed a set of exercises, the Ingredients, to work with the aspects of being sexual that are not about arousal. Examples of the Ingredients include Vibrating, Rolling, Rocking, and Shaking. When a woman is being sexual, her body may experience any one of these movements. By learning, for example, to purposely vibrate and to feel the spreading sensations of the vibrations in her body, she helps pave the way for sexual arousal.

The exercises are often fun. Yet, at first they can be unnerving or awkward. With support and practice women can discover the joy of experiencing the many sensations and dimensions of being in their bodies. The exercises are presented for therapists to give to clients as if they are talking to them directly. Each Ingredient is presented with a goal, preparation, and directions for doing the exercises.

In addition to the Ingredients, there needs to be a progression of body experiences that allows a woman to open up and experience the Ingredients. This progression needs to proceed through a succession of stages that gradually help women to expand their bodies more fully. I call these the Progressive Exercises. For women to be open in more receptive ways, they need to go through the following four stages: Awakening, Awareness, Allowing, and Surrendering. Awakening brings the body to life. Awareness helps her focus and experience her body. Allowing develops and expands her experience. Surrendering involves a full letting go into her experience. Included at each of the four levels are exercises from the Ingredients plus other helpful exercises. For example in the Allowing section the following Ingredients are included: Rolling, Rocking, and Vibrating. In the Surrender section Undulating and Shaking are included. Thus, the Progressive Exercises categorize the Ingredients.

Part IV of the book explores going beyond the Ingredients and the Progressive Exercises. It includes couples exercises, adding in subjective arousal and approaches that work through deeper defenses to sexuality.

If a woman has a partner, she may be ready to share her experiences with him or her. In the chapter on couples I give suggestions for how women can share such experiences as Vibrating and Shaking together with their partners in a safe way that is sometimes quiet and calming and sometimes fun and expanding. This sharing is an important way for a woman to bridge between her individual experience with the exercises in the book and her being close with her partner physically and eventually sexually.

Once a woman has experienced these exercises and feels alive in her body and aware of new sensations, she may be ready to bring sexual arousal into her experience. I use Rosemary Basson's term subjective arousal because it is important that the arousal be in the woman's conscious experience. The Ingredients and the Progressive Exercises have prepared her for the next step in the journey if she wants and is ready to continue. For some women the previous exercises may be enough. Each woman can use whichever parts of this book are helpful to her. For women who are ready to add in subjective arousal, I give suggestions and exercises that in many cases are extensions of what they have already done in the Ingredients and the Progressive Exercises. That is the point: that subjective arousal is part of an overall experience and that it is not isolated making it inaccessible.

There are other therapeutic ways beyond the approach in this book for women to work through the SAS. These methods are not specifically focused on the SAS, but they help women work through their fears of sexuality. Some of the examples I include are cognitive behavioral techniques, self-defense, and visualization. I discuss approaches that bring positive results for women clients in addressing their sexual defenses and in discovering their ability to be sexual. These approaches can be used in addition to the exercises in this book.

OTHER APPROACHES FOR DEALING WITH THE SAS

The Sexual Alarm System is so pervasive that there need to be multiple approaches for dealing with it. What can be done to help women and girls deal with the SAS beyond the approach in this book? What can be done to help girls in their development as sexual beings? What can be done for women who cannot function sexually? What can be done to help women with the many forces that continue to produce the need for the SAS? There are many approaches that can and do help women and girls. They do not address the SAS directly, but they do address the issues that contribute to the SAS. I will discuss books, groups on sexuality for women, programs for teens, programs for men, and more.

Books and Other Media

Books and other media are an effective way to reach a wide audience. There are many resources available for girls, women, parents, educators, and mental health professionals regarding women's sexuality. Several powerful books are discussed in chapter 6. One important book that belongs in this current chapter is Levin and Kilbourne's (2008) book *So Sexy So Soon: The New Sexualized Childhood and What Parents Can Do to Protect Their Kids*. In this book there are two chapters for parents giving them guidelines for how to deal with their young girls and adolescents. Among the authors' suggestions are the following:

> Protect children as much as possible from exposure to sexual imagery and related content in the media and popular culture. (p. 164)
> Establish safe channels for talking about sexual development and related issues with your children. (p. 167)
> Help your teenagers process the sexual images and other media messages they see. (p. 168)

Ask your child's school to take seriously its vital role in working with children and families to counteract the harm caused by the sexualization of children. (p. 172)

Jean Kilbourne's (2002 and 2010) DVDs *Killing Us Softly* 3 and *Killing Us Softly* 4 are available at libraries and would be an excellent way for mothers (and fathers) to start a discussion with their daughters *and* their sons. Males need to learn about these issues also. Her DVD could also be used for classrooms, women's groups, and other learning settings. There are other books and media available such as Mary Pipher's *Reviving Ophelia: Saving the Selves of Adolescent Girls* and Carolyn Davis's (2011) *100 Questions and Answers about Your Daughter's Sexual Wellness and Development*.

Groups on Sexuality for Women

There are many types of groups for women that help deal with the issues related to the SAS. Some of these groups are therapy groups focused on sexual issues. Some are workshops that educate and empower women about their sexuality. An example is the work of Gina Ogden, a psychologist and Diplomate Certified Sex Therapist. She runs a workshop called "Our Sexual Stories: Healing the Wounds, Celebrating the Joy."

Here is an excerpt from the description of this workshop:

> The route to sexual pleasure and intimacy is like the route to any other of life's deep mysteries. It's an exploration of new emotional landscapes. It means opening your wild, precious, vulnerable self to nature, divine presence, and the profound wisdom of your body. It means daring to know what you want. During this workshop for women of all ages and sexual and spiritual orientations, we'll create a safe, confidential environment where you can learn innovative ways to create heart-to-heart communication, expand your capacity for love, creativity, and compassion, transcend guilt, shame, and "good-girls-don't" messages, and heal the sexual wounds of violence, abuse, and compulsivity. (Ogden, 2011)

There are many sex therapists who run workshops for women to help them overcome sexual oppression and inhibition. The power of women coming together to heal is palpable. In the many workshops I have run for women, we could all feel the outpouring of emotion and the full energy of healing from sharing the journey together. Other sex therapists who run groups and workshops for women can be found on the website for the American Association of Sex Educators, Counselors and Therapists (http://aasect.org).

Group Support and Education for Girls and Women

There are any number of programs that educate girls and young women about their sexuality, their bodies, and related issues such as eating disorders and media denigration of women. These programs do not address the SAS per se, but they address many of the issues that contribute to the SAS. These programs educate and teach ways for women to speak up for themselves and to others. Below are examples of several types of programs.

Programs Cited on Jean Kilbourne's Website

In chapter 6 Jean Kilbourne's work on the effects of advertising on women and girls is discussed. The primary effects are the portrayal of women as sexual objects used for selling products. Women's bodies are depicted as uncharacteristically thin, idealized, and unreal. This contributes to the pressures on girls to form their bodies into this distorted ideal and to dissociate from the bodies they have and are developing. Jean Kilbourne's (2011) website cites an extensive resource list of books, articles, agencies, and programs to help girls and women counter these effects. One such program is the True Body Project. The mission of the project is as follows. "The True Body Project proposes to empower girls to identify and stay in their true bodies and maintain and grow their authentic voices" (*True Body Project*, 2011). This project in Cincinnati, Ohio runs classes that help women and girls feel better about themselves by practicing five disciplines. Participants are asked to move, create, see, act, and document. Through these disciplines, participants learn to be in their bodies, discuss the media's portrayal of women, advocate for girls' and women's safety and health, and document their experiences in writing and on film. This kind of support for girls working together is key to building self-esteem and the courage to reject socio-cultural pressures.

Another project referenced in Jean Kilbourne's website is the Real Women Project. This project features a number of goals including, "Help women realize and celebrate their inherent beauty, dignity and capacity for transformation" (*Real Women Project*, 2011). In addition they aim to get rid of negative images of women and replace them with positive empowering images that build self-esteem. The project has created nude sculptures of women of all ages. These sculptures are part of a traveling exhibit that is shown across the country in museums such as the Museum of Science in Boston. The sculptures consist of thirteen images of real women ranging from ages 14 to 66. The same size as the Barbie doll, they were created to provide evidence of the real bodies women have rather than the idealized and impossible body of Barbie. The project has also created a CD of women's stories narrated by the well-known storyteller Alyce Smith Cooper. These stories come from real women about their experiences and struggles about their body image. The CD is meant to be used as a catalyst for women to share their stories with each other. The work of the Real Women Project has been featured in numerous articles in newspapers and magazines such as the *Los Angeles Times* and *People* magazine. Visiting their website is inspirational.

Programs from the Wellesley Centers for Women

This center runs many research, training, and intervention programs related to girls' and women's development and sexuality. Examples of programs they run include: Middle School Bullying & Sexual Violence: Measurement Issues & Etiological Models, Raising Confident and Competent Girls: How Schools Can Support Girls, and Sexual Harassment Policies: Zero Tolerance. The second program, Raising Confident and Competent Girls: How Schools can Support Girls, grew out of research on middle school girls who were African American, Caucasian, Chinese American, and Puerto Rican. The program is described as a research in action program "which offers a range of resources for middle school educators, parents and youth-service providers including presentations and workshops, consultation, needs assessments, program evaluation and training of workshop facilitators" (*Wellesley Centers for Women,* 2011). These groups were informed on such issues as how middle school girls' needs affect their education, how to build girls' self-confidence, and how adults can provide support to girls in early adolescence.

Other programs the center sponsors include women's human rights and gender violence. An example of a research program in the area of gender violence is the Development and Evaluation of Sexual Violence/Harassment Prevention Programs, which is described as follows:

> This study is designed to help increase the capacity of programs to prevent sexual violence and harassment. The long-term goal/objective of this study is to help prevent intimate partner violence, sexual violence, and sexual harassment by employing the most rigorous methods to evaluate strategies for altering the violence-supportive attitudes and norms of youth. (*Wellesley Centers for Women,* 2011)

Within the Wellesley Centers for Women is the Jean Baker Miller Training Institute. The work of the institute is based on the psychology of women developed by Dr. Miller. Chapter 6 describes her work, which focuses on the strengths of women including their strong affiliation with others and their ability to cooperate. Below is a description of the institute.

> The *Jean Baker Miller Training Institute (JBMTI)* at the Wellesley Centers for Women is the home of Relational-Cultural Theory (RCT) which posits that people grow through and toward relationships throughout the lifespan. The Institute is dedicated to enlarging our understanding of human connections and

enhancing human possibility. We examine both the personal and social factors that lead to painful disconnections; and we seek ways to increase our capacity to find strength and facilitate social change by building respectful and encouraging connections. Our work, which focuses on relationship development, has been applied in clinical settings as well as in organizations and has been hailed by some as a transformative model of human potential. (*Wellesley Centers for Women*, 2011)

Baker Miller's work has been expanded by a collaborative group of women who have written extensively on many aspects of RCT, including clinical, organization, and social ramifications and applications of the theory. The Institute runs a variety of programs including a four-day intensive to learn about RCT and its applications, online webinars, lectures, and lunch time seminars. These programs are geared for professionals who can use RCT in their research and work. Programs like these from the Wellesley Centers are vital for girls and women to develop positive body images, to prevent sexual violence against females, and to educate people about female strengths.

Eating Disorders Programs for Girls and Women

There are an increasing number of programs for women and girls addressing eating disorders. Eating disorders are one of the primary outcomes of the pressures for females to measure up to an impossible standard of beauty and thinness. The pressure begins early with girls dieting unnecessarily at a young age into adolescence. Margo Maine (2009) writes, "Eating disorders are now the third most common illness among adolescent females living in the United States, with an incidence as high as 5 percent" (p. 63). Eating disorder clinics run extensive programs for girls and women with overeating disorders, anorexia, and bulimia. Girls are taught nutrition and are educated about the pressures to be thin. They work on their family issues and often on their quest to be perfect. An example of such a program is the Eating Disorders Program for Adolescents at Children's Hospital Boston. The program is for boys and girls, although the vast majority of youths with eating disorders are girls. The program involves a mental health and nutritional evaluation. Treatment may include individual and family therapy, medical monitoring, and/or nutritional support. Each adolescent has an individualized program that may address body image and self-esteem issues as well as other possible coexisting issues such as depression, substance abuse, and obsessive-compulsive disorder. The program works with other eating disorders programs such as the Massachusetts Eating Disorders Association (MEDA), "an eating disorders support network and resource for clients, loved ones, clinicians, educators and the general public . . . [that] is dedicated to the prevention and treatment of eating disorders" (*Children's Hospital Boston,* 2011). Eating disorders programs are sorely needed to address a health crisis for girls and women, a crisis that directly feeds into the Sexual Alarm System.

School Programs for Girls Only

Recognizing that girls lose their voices and that in coed classes they are often overshadowed by boys, there have been any number of programs, particularly in math and science, that have been developed for girls only. These programs have in some cases been controversial. What do girls in such programs learn that is related to the SAS? They learn that they don't have to take a backseat to boys, that on their own and with the support of other girls they can find their strengths and develop their skills. This confidence is part of what is necessary to address the SAS.

One such program is the Coastal Studies for Girls, a semester long science residential program in Freeport, Maine. Their website describes the program:

> Coastal Studies for Girls is a semester-long science and leadership school for tenth grade girls. The school brings girls from around the country to the coast of Maine for 16 weeks during either the fall or spring term of their sophomore year of high school, enabling them to immerse themselves in a challenging and rewarding experience while living in a beautiful coastal landscape that serves as a natural laboratory. . . . As the only residential semester science school in the country that offers a single-gender setting, CSG promotes girls' aspirations in the sciences—a field in which research tells us that girls will excel if they are given consistent and purposeful encouragement. CSG's strong sense of community and dedicated faculty are crucial components in nurturing students' intellectual curiosity, confidence, leadership and self-determination.
>
> *(Coastal Studies for Girls,* 2011)

Girls come from Maine, Boston, New York, etc., to this special program to dedicate themselves to learning science together. Programs such as this seek to build girls' skills, competence, and self-esteem, factors that contribute to dealing with the SAS.

Programs for Girls and Boys

It is vital that boys and men also learn about the SAS and how they contribute to it. The Unitarian Universalist Church has an excellent coed program called Our Whole Lives. Below is a description of the program from their website.

> *Our Whole Lives* is a series of sexuality education curricula for six age groups: grades K–1, grades 4–6, grades 7–9, grades 10–12, young adults (ages 18–35), and adults. Our Whole Lives helps participants make informed and responsible

decisions about their sexual health and behavior. It equips participants with accurate, age-appropriate information in six subject areas: human development, relationships, personal skills, sexual behavior, sexual health, and society and culture. Grounded in a holistic view of sexuality, *Our Whole Lives* not only provides facts about anatomy and human development, but also helps participants clarify their values, build interpersonal skills, and understand the spiritual, emotional, and social aspects of sexuality. (*Unitarian Universalists Association,* 2011)

An example of an exercise from their program for participants in grades 7–9 shows how the program helps boys and girls deal with the SAS. A set of cards, each of which has one intimate and/or sexual behavior with its definition, is placed face down on a table. Participants are given a sheet called the "Sexual Behaviors Continuum." At the top it reads, "I would participate in this behavior with" followed by a list of types of relationships such as, "Someone I am casually dating" and "Someone with whom I am in a committed relationship" or "spouse." One participant picks a card and reads the word(s) and the definition. Participants can ask questions of the leaders. They then write down the behavior on their continuum sheet choosing under which kinds of relationships it belongs for them. For example, a participant might write the item "receive oral sex" under, "someone with whom I am in a committed relationship" and not under "someone I just met" (we would hope). This process is repeated with more cards. The sheets are then used as a springboard for a group discussion to explore these issues. The facilitators are trained to guide the participants to think about the meaning of intimate and sexual acts in their lives. The goal is for young people to become knowledgeable about intimate/sexual behavioral choices and how to make them. This helps girls and boys become aware of boundaries and unsafe behaviors. The values of the Our Whole Lives program are to develop self-worth, sexual health, responsibility, and justice and inclusivity. Parents are very involved in the program and are trained as facilitators. The UUA program is a model program for youth sexual development.

Programs for Men

Men are potential allies for women in addressing male behaviors that contribute to the SAS. Men have wives, partners, sisters, mothers, grandmothers, and daughters who are affected by male behaviors that create the need for the SAS. These issues are addressed in the chapter for men. If men can support women and encourage other men to stop the behaviors that frighten, threaten, and harm women, everybody gains since the SAS negatively affects men also. There are numerous programs for men to help stop sexual violence against women. One such program is Men Can Stop Rape. The program is described on their website as follows:

Though the majority of violent acts against women are committed by men, the vast majority of prevention efforts are risk-reduction and self-defense tactics directed at women. The founders wanted to shift the responsibility of deterring harm away from women by promoting healthy, nonviolent masculinity. Their vision offered a plan for prevention that outlines positive, proactive solutions to engaging men as allies. . . . More than a decade later, Men Can Stop Rape continues to mentor male youth and successfully mobilize them to prevent men's violence against women and other men . . . (*Men Can Stop Rape*, 2011)

The program runs trainings, workshops, lectures, and leadership training. One of their groups is the Men of Strength Club, a program designed to mobilize young men to prevent sexual and dating violence. It is very encouraging to visit their website and read about their work to develop men as allies for women in the fight against sexual violence of women. Other such programs include Men Against Sexual Violence (*Men Against Sexual Violence*, 2011) and *One in Four* (2011), which run men's programs to help prevent sexual violence and assist women who have experienced rape. Seeing men stand up for women and address other men about women's issues is truly inspirational.

Equality for Women and the SAS

Recently *Newsweek* (September 26, 2011) ran a cover story about the status of women across the world. They compared the status of women in many countries on a number of important dimensions: education, health, justice, and economic status. It is striking that the women in the lowest ranking countries often experience a far greater degree of sexual exploitation including rape, childhood marriage, and female genital mutilation. It is reported, for example, that in Chad, "Women have almost no legal rights, and many marriages are arranged when the girls are 11 or 12" (p. 32) and that in Pakistan, "Marital rape is not illegal, there were almost 800 honor killings in 2010, and violence against women is up 20 percent this year" (p. 32). There appears to be a direct relationship between greater legal, social, and economic equality and opportunity and sexual and physical treatment of women. The greater a woman's independence and freedom, the greater control she has over her sexuality. This is not news, yet it is startling. It does not mean that in the top-ranked countries women have no SAS and there is no sexual exploitation of women. We have yet to achieve a society free of sexual oppression of women.

Title IX was a landmark legislation that made an enormous contribution to women's equality. It is a law that stated that no person on the basis of sex could be subject to discrimination in any educational program or activity that received federal funding. Further defining of the law mandated that colleges and universities must provide equal opportunity in sports programs for men and women. This revolutionized sports programs across the country. Where there were none before, now there were women's rowing teams and women's basketball teams. Throughout colleges, universities, and down to high schools and middle schools, girls and women began to participate in sports in record numbers. Think of the impact this has on women participants' body image, confidence, and ability to deal with the SAS! Although these programs do not target the SAS directly, they help women be in their bodies, feel in charge of their bodies, and develop physical strength, all things that help manage and diminish the SAS. Women's professional sports is now a major phenomenon. Think of the names Hope Solo, Mia Hamm, Serena Williams . . . now household names. These are heroes that girls can look to and admire, providing an alternative to the models of unattainable sexiness and beauty of supermodels such as Giselle Bundchen.

Women's Health

Important advances in medicine and specifically sexual medicine are helpful with the Sexual Alarm System. Twenty years ago no one had heard of vulvodynia. Many have still not heard of it. This is a condition in which girls and women have pain at the entrance to their vagina, making sexual intercourse and some kinds of touch painful. Women often blame themselves for the pain believing that it is their fault and that there is something wrong with them. They avoid sex and/or endure the pain. Doctors told women that the pain was in their head (and some uninformed doctors still say this). Now we know that vulvodynia is a real physical condition. The physical cause is still unknown. Today there are a number of physical treatments available including use of lidocaine, physical therapy, trigger point injections, and biofeedback. Woman with vulvodynia can learn to decrease or eliminate their pain and together with their partners develop a positive sexual experience. The presence of vulvodynia, like any vulvar pain, adds to a woman's SAS. Therapeutic treatment helps decrease the heightened presence of the Alarm. For more information on vulvodynia go to http://www.nva.org (National Vulvodynia Association).

There is controversy about some of the advances in women's health, for example regarding childbirth and menopause. Many believe that the "medicalization" of women's health has decreased women's control over their bodies. It is argued, for example, that medicine sees menopause as a disease rather than as a normal passage in a woman's life. Women have been barraged with medical solutions such as hormone replacement therapy (HRT) only to be told, after taking HRT for years, that research finds it causes any number of health risks. Suddenly hordes of women were calling their doctors and going off of HRT. Hot flashes, mental confusion, sleep issues returned. What to do? Slowly women are taking menopause back as their own. Given the ups and downs of medical advice, more peri-menopausal and menopausal women are questioning and learning information about their bodies. They are considering their doctor's advice, reading, talking to each other, and making more informed choices. They are seeing menopause as a natural occurrence not to be dreaded, but to be handled with care. Christiane Northrup (2006) in her book *The Wisdom of Menopause* refers to hot flashes as "power surges" (p. 129). We still have a long way to go for women to feel empowered in dealing with menopause let alone in dealing with the effects of aging on sexuality. The more women take charge of their bodies, the more they can control their sexuality and their Sexual Alarm System.

The book *Our Bodies Ourselves* by the Boston Women's Health Book Collective (2011) has been through nine editions and has been printed in many countries around the world, including such countries as Albania, Tibet, and Thailand. The Collective describes their work as follows:

> Our Bodies Ourselves (OBOS), also known as the Boston Women's Health Book Collective (BWHBC), is a nonprofit, public interest women's health education, advocacy, and consulting organization. Beginning in 1970 with the publication of the first edition of *Our Bodies, Ourselves*, OBOS has inspired the women's health movement by:
>
> - Producing books that make accurate health and medical information accessible to a broad audience by weaving women's stories into a framework of practical, clearly written text
> - Identifying and collaborating with exemplary individuals and organizations that provide services, generate research and policy analysis, and organize for social change
> - Inspiring and empowering women to become engaged in the political aspects of sustaining good health for themselves and their communities
>
> (Boston Women's Health Collective, 2005)

This book has had a major impact on women's access to information about their bodies and on women's views about their health and sexuality. It helped to start a movement that continues today with women taking more control of their health and sexuality. The group now is involved in many new areas such as health policy, other publications, and health projects such as the Latina Health Initiative, which is described as follows.

> The Latina Health Initiative is an ongoing project of Our Bodies Ourselves that addresses health education and information needs of Latinas. Our goal for this project is to provide opportunities for outreach, prevention awareness, and network-building in Spanish-speaking communities locally, nationally and internationally. (*Our Bodies Ourselves*, 2011)

Access to better health care and health information helps women become more empowered in their bodies. This feeds into diminishing the unwanted effects of the SAS.

Famous Women Advocating for Women

There are numerous famous women who use their voices, their influence, and their ability to raise money and organize to help women gain more rights, become more educated, become more empowered, gain skills, improve economically, and gain more influence. Oprah is certainly one of the most prominent women who is well known for her work to help girls and women. Her TV programs have included segments on sexual abuse, domestic violence, eating disorders, and many other subjects of benefit to women. The Women's Conference writes of her work:

> To date, the Oprah's Angel Network has raised more than $80 million to help educate and empower women and children to believe in themselves, to support people around the globe in pursuing their dreams . . . and to provide those who are underprivileged and underserved with the means and education to reach their potential. In addition, she has developed programs in Africa for girls, for the violated, and for those afflicted by AIDS. In 2007, she opened the Oprah Winfrey Leadership Academy for Girls in South Africa. Her goal is to educate and empower a new generation of women to help lead sub-Saharan Africa towards peace and economic prosperity . . . Oprah Winfrey has influenced the way women think, talk, eat, study, shop, exercise and lead. She has changed our every day culture and vernacular to include respect for the emotional and spiritual. (*Women's Conference*, 2011)

Hillary Clinton is another very prominent woman who tirelessly promotes causes for women. At the 1995 Fourth World Conference on Women, when her husband was president, Hillary ascended the world stage and put women's rights at the forefront by saying that women's rights are a human rights issue. As secretary of state:

> she pushes for recognition of women's contributions in traditional areas such as health and education, along with newer and, in her view, equally critical arenas such as diplomacy and peacekeeping. "Politics is seen in most societies, including our own, I would add, as a largely male sport—unarmed combat— and women are very often ignored or pushed aside in an effort to gain or consolidate power," she says. Her work aims to change that. (*The Daily Beast*, 2011)

Hillary helps sponsor programs to develop gender equality, she pushes world leaders on women's rights, and she follows up on issues that she cares about. "'I honestly think Hillary Clinton wakes up every day thinking about how to improve the lives of women and girls,' says Theresa Loar. 'And I don't know another world leader who is doing that'" (*The Daily Beast*, 2011).

Oprah and Hillary are just two of the most well-known women who use their influence and money to help women with issues vital to their empowerment, their sexuality, and the quality of their lives. Another such woman includes well-known designer Diane von Furstenberg, who has established the DVF awards to honor women whose work has helped transform the lives of women.

SUMMARY

Much is being done to help women find their authentic selves, their true bodies, their power and independence socially and economically. Around the world there are clinics, support groups, mentoring programs, and education for women and for men about women. This chapter describes some of the exciting efforts to help women become freer of oppression in general and sexual oppression in particular. Yet, every day we read and hear about a woman being sexually assaulted and killed by her partner. Every day we see impossible models of female beauty that alienate women and girls from their bodies and lead to such issues as eating disorders. This book is one of the many efforts to help women find themselves, their bodies, their power. We must keep going on this life-changing journey that will free us all!

Bibliography

Anand, M. (1989). *The art of sexual ecstasy*. New York: Penguin Putnam.

Anand, M. (1996). *The art of sexual magic*. New York: Penguin Putnam.

Apfelbaum, B. (1995). Masters and Johnson revisited: A case of desire disparity. In R. C. Rosen & S. Lieblum (Eds.), *Case studies in sex therapy*. New York: Guilford Press.

Arreola, S. G. (2005). Latino/a childhood sexuality. In M. Asencio (Ed.). *Latina/o sexualities*. (pp. 48–61). New Brunswick, NJ: Rutgers University Press.

Babior, S. & Goldman, C. (1996). *Panic, anxiety & phobias: New strategies to free yourself from worry and fear*. Duluth, MN: Pfiefer-Hamilton.

Barbach, L. (1983). *For each other*. New York: Penguin Putnam

Barbach, L. (2000). *For yourself*. New York: Penguin Putnam

Baker Miller, J. (1986). *Toward a new psychology of women, 2nd ed*. Boston: Beacon Press.

Barlow, D. H. & Cerny, J. A. (1988). *Psychological treatment of panic*. New York: The Guilford Press.

Barlow, D. H. & Craske, M. G. (2007). *Mastery of your anxiety and panic: Workbook (treatments that work)*. New York: Oxford University Press.

Basson, R. (2007). Sexual desire/arousal disorders in women. In. S. Lieblum (Ed.), *Principles and practice of sex therapy, 4th ed*. (pp. 25–53). New York: Guilford Press.

Benson, H. (2000). *The relaxation response*. New York: HarperCollins.

Berk, L. E. (2006). *Childhood development*. Boston: Allyn & Bacon.

Berman, J. & Berman, L. (2005). *For women only*. New York: Henry Holt and Company.

Blackledge, C. (2004). *The story of V: A natural history of female sexuality*. New Brunswick, NJ: Rutgers University Press.

Boston Women's Health Collective. (2005). *Our bodies, ourselves: A new edition for a new era*. New York: Touchstone.

Breath of fire. Retrieved October 29, 2011, from http://www.youtube.com/watch?v= CB7v3tHow-o

Brown, L. M. & Gilligan, C. (1992). *Meeting at the crossroads: Women's psychology and girls' development*. Cambridge, MA: Harvard University Press.

Butler, R. N. & Lewis, M. I. (2002). *The new love and sex after 60*. New York: Ballantine Books.

Cambridge Women's Pornography Cooperative & Anderson, S. (2007). *Porn for women*. San Francisco: Chronicle Books, LLC.

Canadian foundation for trauma research and education. Retrieved December 4, 2010, from http://www.cftre.com/srt.php.

Charlton, R. S. & Brigel, F. W. (1997). Treatment of arousal and orgasmic disorders. In R. S. Charlton (Ed.), *Treating sexual disorders* (pp. 237–80). San Francisco: Jossey-Bass.

175

Charlton, R. S. & Quatman, T. (1997). A therapist's guide to the physiology of sexual response. In R. S. Charlton (Ed.), *Treating sexual disorders* (pp.29–58). San Francisco: Jossey-Bass.

Children's hospital Boston. Retrieved October 14, 2011, from http://www.childrenshospital/clinicalservices.

Coastal studies for girls. Retrieved October 13, 2011, from http://coastalstudiesforgirls.org.

Davis, C. F. (2011). *100 questions and answers about your daughter's sexual wellness and development* . Sudbury, MA: Jones and Bartlett Publishers.

D'Emilio, J. & Freedman, E. B. (1997). *Intimate Matters: A history of sexuality in America, 2nd ed.* New York: Harper & Row Publishers.

Dodson, B. (1996). *Sex for one: The joy of selfloving.* New York: Three Rivers Press.

Flexnor, E. & Fitzpatrick, E. (1996). *Century of struggle: The woman's rights movement in the United States.* Cambridge, MA: The Belknap Press of Harvard University.

Friday, N. (1977). *My mother myself.* New York: Delacourte Press.

Gilligan, C. (1982. *In a different voice: Psychological theory and women's development.* Cambridge, MA: Harvard University Press.

Goldstein, A. & Brandon, M. (2004). *Reclaiming desire.* Emmaus, PA: Rodale.

Goleman, D. (2006). *Emotional intelligence.* New York: Bantam Dell.

Hawthorne, N. (2010). *The scarlet letter.* New York: Tribeca Books.

Heiman, J. (2007). Orgasmic disorders in women. In S. Lieblum (Ed.), *Principles and practices of sex therapy, 4th ed.* (pp. 84–123). New York: Guilford Press.

Heiman, J. & LoPiccolo, J. (1988). *Becoming orgasmic: A sexual and personal growth program for women.* New York: Prentice Hall Press.

Herman, J. (1997). *Trauma and recovery.* New York: Harper Collins.

Jones Goodwin, A. & Agronin, M. E. (1997). *A woman's guide to overcoming sexual fear and pain.* Oakland, CA: New Harbinger Publications.

Kabat-Zinn, J. (2005). *Coming to our senses.* New York: Hyperion.

Kilbourne, J. *Jean Kilbourne.* Retrieved October 17, 2011, from http://www.jeankilbourne.com.

Kilbourne, J. (2002). *Killing us softly 3: Advertising's image of women.* Northampton, MA: Media Education Foundation.

Kilbourne, J. (2010). *Killing us softly 4: Advertising's image of women.* Northampton, MA: Media Education Foundation.

Kinsey, A. et al. (1953). *Sexual behavior in the human female.* Philadelphia: W. B. Saunders.

Levin, D. E. & Kilbourne, J. (2008) *So sexy so soon: The new sexualized childhood and what parents can do to protect their kids.* New York: Ballantine Books.

Levin, D. E. (2009). So sexy so soon: The sexualization of childhood. In S. Olfman (Ed.), *The sexualization of childhood* (pp. 75–88). Westport, CT: Praeger.

Lieblum, S.R. (2007). *Principles and practices of sex therapy, 4th ed.* New York: Guilford Press.

Loulan, J. (1984). *Lesbian sex.* Duluth. MN: Spinsters Ink.

Lowen, A. (1994). *Bioenergetics: The revolutionary therapy that uses the language of the body to heal the problems of the mind.* New York: Penguin Books.

Lowen, A. & Lowen, L. (1997). *The way to vibrant health: A manual of bioenergetic exercises.* New York: Harper Colophon Books.

Maine, M. (2009). Something's happening here: Sexual objectification, body image distress, and eating disorders. In S. Olfman (Ed.), *The sexualization of childhood* (pp. 63–74). Westport, CT: Praeger.

Maltz, W. (Ed.) (2003). *Intimate kisses: The poetry of sexual pleasure.* Novato, CA: New World Library.

Maltz, W. (Ed.). (2007). *Passionate hearts: The poetry of sexual love, 2nd ed.* Novato, CA: New World Library.

Maltz, W. & Maltz, L. (2010). *The porn trap: The essential guide to overcoming problems caused by pornography.* New York: Harper Paperback.

Maltz, W. & Boss, S. (2008). *Private thoughts: Exploring the power of women's sexual fantasies.* Charleston, SC: Booksurge.

Maltz, W. (2012). *The sexual healing journey: A guide for survivors of sexual abuse, 3rd ed.* New York: HarperCollins Publishers.

Masters, W. & Johnson, V. (1970). *Human sexual inadequacy.* Boston: Little, Brown and Company.

McCarthy, B. W. & Metz, M. E. (2008). *Men's sexual health: Fitness for satisfying sex.* New York: Routledge.

McCarthy, B. W. & McCarthy, E. J. (2003). *Rekindling desire: A step by step program to help low-sex and no-sex marriages.* New York: Taylor Francis Books.

McGoldrick, M., Loonan, R. & Wohlsifer, D. (2007). Sexuality and culture. In S. Lieblum (Ed.), *Principles and practices of sex therapy, 4th ed.* (pp. 416–441). New York: Guilford Press.

Men against sexual violence. Retrieved October 18, 2011, from http://pcar.org/men-against-sexual-violence-masv.

Men can stop rape. Retrieved October 17, 2011, from http://www.mencanstoprape.org.

Merriam-Webster dictionary. Retrieved October 29, 2011, from http://www.merriam-webster.com.

Mersky Leder, J. (1991). *Brothers and sisters: How they shape our lives.* New York: St. Martin's Press.

Model mugging. Retrieved December 4, 2010, from http://www.modelmugging.org.

Muir, G. (2008). *Yang style traditional long form t'ai chi ch'uan: As taught by Master T.T. Liang.* Berkeley, CA: Blue Snake Books.

National Vulvodynia Association. Retrieved October 18, 2011, from http://www.nva.org.

Northrup, C. (2005). *Mother-daughter wisdom: Creating a legacy of physical and emotional health.* New York: Random Dell.

Northrup, C. (2006). *The wisdom of menopause.* New York: Bantam.

Nottage, L. (2010). *Ruined.* New York: Dramatists Play Service.

Ochs, R. & Rowley, S. E. (Eds.). (2005). *Getting bi: Voices of bisexuals around the world.* Boston: Bisexual Resource Center.

Ogden, G. *Expanding sex therapy.* Retrieved October 18, 2011, from http://www.expandingsextherapy.com.

Ogden, G. (2008). *The return of desire.* Boston: Trumpeter Books.

Ogden, G. (2006). *The heart and soul of sex: Making the isis connection.* Boston: Trumpeter Books.

Ogden, G. (2007). *Women who love sex: Ordinary women describe their paths to pleasure, intimacy and ecstasy.* Boston: Trumpeter Books.

Olfman, S. (Ed.). (2009). *The sexualization of childhood.* Westport, CT: Praeger.

Olfman, S. (2009). "The sexualization of childhood: Growing older younger/growing younger older." In S. Olfman (Ed.), *The sexualization of childhood* (pp. 1–6). Westport, CT: Praeger.

One in four. Retrieved October 17, 2011, from http://oneinfourusa.org.

Our bodies ourselves. Retrieved October 17, 2011, from http://www.ourbodiesourselves.org.

Pipher, M. (2004). *Reviving Ophelia: Saving the selves of adolescent girls.* New York: G.P. Putnam's Sons.

Rako, S. (1996). *The hormone of desire: The truth about testosterone, sexuality and menopause.* New York: Three Rivers Press.

Ramsdale, D. & Ramsdale, E. (1991). *Sexual energy ecstasy.* New York: Bantam Books.

Real women project. Retrieved October 10, 2011, from http://www.realwomenproject.org.

Reed Gach, M. (1997). *Acupressure for lovers.* New York: Bantam Books.

Rosenberg, J. L. (1977). *Total orgasm.* New York: Wildwood House.

Rygh, J. & Sanderson, W. C. (2004). *Treating generalized anxiety disorder.* New York: Guilford Press.

Savin-Williams, R. C. (1997). Self labeling and disclosure among gay, lesbian, and bisexual youth. In J. Laird & R. J. Green (Eds.), *Lesbians and gays in couples and families: A handbook for therapists.* (pp. 153–182). San Francisco: Jossey-Bass Publishers.

Schnarch, D. (1991). *Constructing the sexual crucible.* New York: W. W. Norton & Company.

Schwartz, P. & Rutter, V. (1998). *The gender of sexuality.* London: Pine Forge Press.

Secunda, V. (1992). *Women and their fathers.* New York; Delacorte Press.

Singer Kaplan, N. (1979). *Disorders of sexual desire: And other new concepts and techniques in sex therapy*. New York: Brunner/Mazel Publishers.

Singer Kaplan, H. (1974). *The new sex therapy*. New York: Brunner/Mazel Publishers.

Schnarch, D. M. (1991). *Constructing the sexual crucible: An integration of sexual and marital therapy*. New York: W. W. Norton & Company.

Stendhal, R. (2003). *True secrets of lesbian desire*. Berkeley, CA: North Atlantic Books.

Stewart. E. (2005). *The V book: A doctor's guide to complete vulvovaginal health*. New York: Bantam Books.

Strong, B., Yarber, W. L., Sayad, B. W. & DeVault, C. (2008) *Human sexuality*. Boston: McGraw Hill.

The continuum complete international encyclopedia of sexuality. Retrieved October 29, 2011, from http://www.kinseyinstitute.org/ccies/

The daily beast. Retrieved October 16, 2011, from http:// thedailybeast.com.

The free dictionary. Retrieved August 28, 2010, from http://www.thefreedictionary.com/instinct.

The 2011 global women's progress report. *Newsweek*. (pp. 27–33). September 26, 2011.

Tolman, D. L. (2002). *Dilemmas of desire*. Cambridge, MA: Harvard University Press.

True body project. Retrieved October 10, 2011, from http://www.truebodyproject.org.

Tuana, N. (1993). *The less noble sex*. Indianapolis: Indiana University Press.

Unitarian universalists association. Retrieved October 17, 2011, from http://www.uua.org.

Vanity Fair, August 1991, v.54, n. 8.

Weeks, G. R., Odell, M. & Methven, S. (2005). *If only I had known: Avoiding common mistakes in couples therapy*. New York: W. W. Norton & Company.

Weeks, G. R. & Treat, S. (2001). *Couples in treatment*. New York: Routledge.

Weitz, R. (2010). *The politics of women's bodies*. New York: Oxford University Press.

Wellesley centers for women. Retrieved October 12 & 14, 2011, from http://wcwonline.org.

Women's conference. Retrieved October 19, 2011, from http://www.womensconference.org.

Women's self defense institute. Retrieved December 4, 2010, from http://www.self-defense-mind-body-spirit.com.

Wyatt, G. E. (1997). *Stolen women: Reclaiming our sexuality, taking back our lives*. New York: John Wiley & Sons.

Zilbergeld, B. (1999). *The new male sexuality*. New York: Bantam Books.

Index

179

About the Author

Dr. Judy Leavitt is a licensed psychologist and Diplomate Certified Sex Therapist. She has a private practice in Wayland, Mass., where she works with individuals, couples, and families. At the Massachusetts School of Professional Psychology in Boston, Mass., she is an adjunct faculty teaching Human Sexuality and Couples Therapy. For many years she taught at the Smith School of Social Work. In addition she worked as a senior family business consultant at Transition Consulting Group for fifteen years. She often speaks at mental health centers, hospitals, and professional conferences such as the Harvard Medical School conference "Aspects of Aging" in 2006 and "Treating Couples" in 2009. In 1993 she was voted as "Teacher of the Year" at Interface in Cambridge, Mass. Dr. Leavitt has also authored a book entitled *Common Dilemmas in Couple Therapy*, published by Routledge in 2009.

CPSIA information can be obtained at www.ICGtesting.com
Printed in the USA
BVOW070756300512

291167BV00001B/5/P